Natural
SOAP

⤳⤳⤳⤳⤳SECOND EDITION⬳⬳⬳⬳⬳

Natural
SOAP
SECOND EDITION

TECHNIQUES & RECIPES FOR BEAUTIFUL
HANDCRAFTED SOAPS, LOTIONS & BALMS

Melinda Coss

IMM lifestyle books™

Read. Learn. Do What You Love.

For Railea, Lily, Kai, Isabel, Leo, Max and Jed — my magnificent seven.

Published 2016—IMM Lifestyle Books
www.IMMLifestyleBooks.com

IMM Lifestyle Books are distributed in the UK by Grantham Book Service,
Trent Road, Grantham, Lincolnshire, NG31 7XQ.

In North America, IMM Lifestyle Books are distributed by
Fox Chapel Publishing, 1970 Broad Street, East Petersburg, PA 17520,
www.FoxChapelPublishing.com.

ISBN 978 1 5048 0062 4
Printed in Singapore

10 9 8 7 6 5 4 3 2 1

The soap recipes in this book are not directly converted from metric to imperial based on 28.35 g per oz but on 25 g per oz. This adjustment was made to the recipes to achieve a safe and easy-to-weigh alternative. Please use either metric or imperial measurements but don't mix the two.

The information in this book has been carefully researched and all efforts have been made to ensure accuracy. The author and publisher accept no responsibility for any injuries, damage or losses incurred either during, or subsequent to, following the instructions in this book.

Contents

INTRODUCTION   6

INGREDIENTS   8

BAR SOAPS   20

The Basics   21

Saponification, Superfatting and Essential Stuff   24

Pure and Gentle   30

Fruit Soaps   38

Scrub Bars   46

Provençal   54

Home Spa   64

Out of Africa   72

Festive Soaps   82

Special Effects   90

LIQUID SOAPS   92

The Basics   92

Recipes   97

CREAMS, BALMS, WHIPS AND MELTS   106

The Basics   106

Making Creams and Lotions   109

Creams   112

Balms   126

Whips and Melts   132

SETTING UP A SOAP MAKING BUSINESS   138

INDEX   142

FURTHER READING   142

RESOURCES   143

Introduction

THE VAST MAJORITY OF MY WORKING life has been spent in the design and marketing of craft products. For many years I was involved in knitting and embroidery and wrote numerous books on those subjects, but in the mid-nineties I discovered soap making and my life was turned completely upside down. It is hard to imagine how a simple bar of soap can fundamentally change lives but history shows that it truly can.

Firstly, if you look at soap as a simple hygiene product it has and does undoubtedly fight disease and save lives. In addition, soap presents creative marketing people with an irresistible blank canvas. They begin with a product that is used by men, women and children worldwide in all their wonderful shapes, colours, sizes and income brackets and create, design and package a simple bar of soap to fulfil needs, lifestyles and aspirations. I am frequently asked the question 'can you really make a living making and selling soap?'. The answer is that 70 per cent of people use soap and the other 30 per cent just need to be persuaded. This is a dream market for an entrepreneur but your success or failure will depend on your business acumen, your creativity, your marketing skills and your product, in that order.

Soap making sent me on the hugely challenging adventure of building an enterprise from scratch with traditional values and methods and with the aim of making enough volume to supply supermarkets. My creative and business learning curve was steep and fruitful, and in the last five years I have had the privilege of sharing that learning curve with entrepreneurial spirits worldwide through my consultancy work and to teach hands-on soap making to the many hundreds of people who have attended my courses.

An even greater privilege has come from the opportunity to start social soapmaking enterprises in Africa and to discover and add value to local plants and oils that can be used in soaps and toiletries. This work has been humbling and hugely satisfying.

If you have my two earlier books *Handmade Soap Book* and *Gourmet Soaps Made Easy* you will note many differences in method in my bar soap section. These changes come from years of experimentation and practical experience. My previous methods still work but the processes suggested in this book will make your life a lot easier.

I am also including sections on liquid soap making and on creams and lotions. Liquid soap outsells bar soap eight to one so if you want to run a business it's a good skill to master. Creams and lotions give you the opportunity of experimenting with all the wonderful luxury oils without worrying about caustic substances – the products you can produce at home in your kitchen are just wonderful but don't take my word for it, make them and see for yourself!

Finally, for those soap entrepreneurs of the future I have included a section on setting up a business.

Enjoy!

Melinda Coss.

Ingredients

SOAP IS THE RESULT OF COMBINING AN alkali with an acid. The alkali used to make bar soap is sodium hydroxide (also known as caustic soda, NaOH and lye) and the alkali used to make liquid and soft soaps is potassium hydroxide. The acid can be any kind of oil or fat, be it animal or vegetable. If you think of all the wonderful plant derived oils and fats that are available you will realize what a huge palette this gives you to play with. In the following section I will explain the virtues of various oils and additives and hopefully help you to make your ideal product.

Creams and lotions are a combination of oils/ fats/butters, water additives and an emulsifier to hold them together. They contain no harsh chemicals and making them is a similar experience to that of making mayonnaise.

Reserve the use of your finest grade base and essential oils for making creams and lotions – here the benefits will really come through.

Once you have your basic product formula there are many ingredients you can use to add colour, texture and fragrance and this section should give you plenty of ideas.

If you think sensibly about the fact that oils are mixed with a caustic solution to create soap, you must also realize that the caustic element will, certainly to some degree, destroy the natural benefits of any chosen oil. For this reason, and for reasons of economy (oils are becoming very costly), it is wise not to invest in top grade refined oils when making soap. Many companies boast the use of 'virgin olive oil' in their products, but in reality 'pomace' (the roughest grade of olive oil produced from the third pressing of the fruit) creates far better soap. Some olive oils sold as 'pomace' are in fact blended so take care to read labels before you buy as you need a 100 per cent olive pomace oil. Essential oils need not be top grade but they should be 100 per cent pure and not blended with alcohol or enhancers. Always buy your ingredients from a reputable supplier (the stockist list on page 143 should help you to find one).

CHOOSE WHAT YOU USE

Sales of natural and pseudo-natural soaps and cosmetics are rising year on year. There are several sound reasons for this, the first being that we live in a world where our tolerance to chemical household products is diminishing and there is a sharp increase in the number of people suffering from skin allergies. The second reason is that any right thinking person wants to do their bit for the environment and to leave a sustainable world behind them for future generations to enjoy. The third reason is a growing awareness that fair trade sales of natural botanical products help to create and sustain agricultural industries so alleviating poverty in under developed countries. What a wonderful product we have here!

In order to meet the growing demand for natural products, many manufacturers choose to express 'naturalness' in their brand names and include minute amounts of botanical oils. The way to beat this trend is to read the label on the package and to be aware of certain ingredients that are widely in use but are in fact proven to be skin irritants, or even worse are carcinogenic. That said, I do not support the argument that 'natural' is, without exception 'good' – we need to make informed decisions on what we buy. Remember that arsenic (as an extreme example) is 100 per cent natural!

If you suffer from eczema or very sensitive skin you should not use products that contain any colourings or fragrance – natural or unnatural – as these are the biggest contributors to skin irritation. Some essential oils (such as Roman chamomile) will help mildly sensitive skin and are safe to use in baby products, but only in very tiny quantities. Some soapmakers, aware that 'no smell means no sell', bombard their products with large quantities of essential oils and whilst the soap may smell divine, doing so is downright dangerous. In the EU, cosmetic legislation dictates that a maximum of 2 per cent essential oils can legally be used in soap products but in fact 1 to 1.5 per cent is a much safer amount to aim for.

When reading the labels on your shop bought soaps and cosmetics, be aware of the following:

Sodium lauryl sulphate (SLS)

This is a detergent derived from coconut oil and is widely used in shampoos. It contains endocrine disruptors and estrogen mimics and it can damage the skin barrier functions, which will increase the allergic response to other toxins and allergens.

Sodium laureth sulfate (SLES)

Found in shampoo, toothpaste, bubble bath, body wash and soap, this is another known

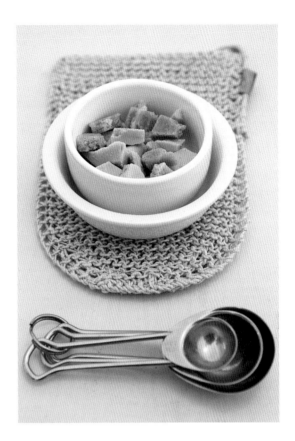

endocrine disruptor and estrogen mimic and it is also carcinogenic. It allows other chemicals to penetrate skin more deeply and potentially enter the bloodstream.

Mineral oil and petroleum jelly

These petroleum-based ingredients block pores, act as barriers and suppress normal skin functions.

Parabens (methylparaben, propylparaben, ethylparaben, butylparaben)

Used to preserve cosmetic products, there is a growing public awareness about the dangers of using parabens and they have been linked to breast cancer. The counter argument is that parabens aren't dangerous at very low levels and they are stable preservatives, protecting products against far more dangerous viruses and villains. On the market are a number of safer preservatives that can be used in your natural products. However despite the regular industry proclamations of the discovery of a wholly natural

DEA (diethanolamine, cocamide DEA, oleamide DEA and lauramide DEA)

These ingredients are used to increase lather in industrially-produced soap and have been known to react with other ingredients to create a carcinogenic that can easily be absorbed by the skin.

Even when using entirely natural oils it is important that you establish where they were grown, and for ecological reasons avoid anything produced in an unsustainable environment. Palm oil is a particular case in question. Used in 1 out of every 10 products on the supermarket shelves and also widely used in bio-fuel, the rush to create palm plantations, particularly in the tropical rainforests of Malaysia and Indonesia, has led to the destruction of forests that support endangered wildlife, particularly tree-dwelling primates. Palm oil is traditionally a soap-making staple and you can buy it from sustainable sources – just make sure you ask your potential supplier the right questions.

OILS, FATS AND BUTTERS

The following list describes the principal properties of a variety of oils, fats and butters that can be used in your products. To help you understand the terminology, the table on page 10 shows what the fatty acids actually contribute to your soaps in terms of quality and feel, and the higher the percentage specified next to the oil, the greater the contribution. The iodine value also contributes to the hardness of a soap bar, but in this case the lower the value the harder the bar.

Oils marked with an asterisk (*) are basic, relatively-affordable soap making oils otherwise known as 'base oils'. The others are quite precious but can be used in small quantities in your soaps. The really expensive oils should be reserved for your cream and lotion recipes.

If an oil is described as being high in anti-oxidants, this means it is full of vitamins, minerals and enzymes that will protect both your skin and the product itself from degeneration.

preservative (such as gse, roe and citricidal), none of these products will pass a challenge test.

Borax (sodium borate)

Widely used in the US to stabilize and thicken liquid soap, the use of Borax is restricted under EU cosmetic legislation as it is a strong irritant. It can cause rashes in babies and young children.

FATTY ACID	PROPERTIES IT LENDS TO SOAP
LAURIC ACID	Hard bar, cleansing, fluffy lather, fast trace
LINOLEIC ACID	Conditioning
MYRISTIC ACID	Hard bar, cleansing, fluffy lather
OLEIC ACID	Conditioning
PALMITIC ACID	Hard bar, stable lather
RICINOLEIC ACID	Conditioning, fluffy stable lather
STEARIC ACID	Hard bar, stable lather

ALMOND OIL (sweet) *
Good base for creams and body oils, high in Omega 9 and vitamins A and B, makes a white bar of soap. Good, inexpensive base for creams and lotions.
INCI: *Prunus dulcis*
Oleic: 64–82%
Linoleic: 8–28%
Palmitic: 6–8%
Iodine: 93–106

APRICOT KERNEL OIL
Good for sensitive, dry and problem skins, has excellent skin softening qualities.
INCI: *Prunus armeniaca*
Oleic: 58–74%
Linoleic: 20–34%
Palmitic: 4–7%
Iodine: 92–108

ARGAN NUT OIL
Rich in antioxidants and vitamin E, an excellent choice for mature or dry skins.
INCI: *Argania spinosa*
Oleic: 42.8%
Linoleic: 36.8%
Palmitic: 12%
Stearic: 6%
Iodine: 98

AVOCADO OIL *
A semi-fatty oil with a high vitamin content. A good choice for problem skins.
INCI: *Persea gratissima*
Oleic: 36–80%
Palmitic: 7–32%
Linoleic: 6–18%
Stearic: 1.5%
Iodine: 82–90

BABASSU OIL *
Properties similar to those in coconut oil with high lauric acid content. Rich and moisturizing.
INCI: *Orbygnia oleifera*
Lauric: 50%

Myristic: 20%
Palmitic: 11%
Oleic: 10%
Stearic: 3.5%
Iodine: 10-20

BAOBAB OIL *
Rich in Omega acids and vitamin D. Creates a barrier that protects the skin.
INCI: *Adansonia digitata*
Palmitic: 24%
Oleic: 36%
Linoleic: 31%
Iodine: 88

BORAGE OIL
High in gama linolenic acid, helps to lock in moisture and smooth the skin. An ideal choice for a baby cream.
INCI: *Borago officinalis*
Palmitic: 10–11%
Oleic: 16–20%
Linoleic: 35–38%
Stearic: 3.5–4.5%
Iodine: 165–185

BLACK CUMIN OIL
Rich in essential fatty acids, good for problem skin and promotes smoothness.
INCI: *Nigella sativa*
Oleic: 64%
Palmitic: 11.7%
Linoleic: 12%
Linolenic: 70%
Iodine: 110–125

CALENDULA OIL
Antiseptic and anti-inflammatory, excellent oil for damaged and sensitive skin.
INCI: *Calendula officinalis*
Calendula oil is made by macerating the flowers in a base oil. Therefore the fatty acid values relate to the specific base oil used, rather than the calendula itself. Check the identity of the base oil with your supplier.

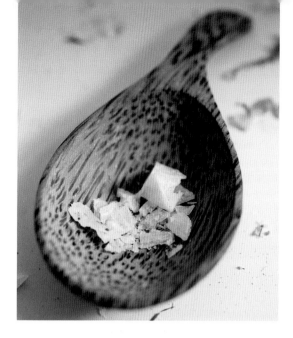

CANOLA OIL *

(A specific variety of rapeseed oil used in the US.)
Used mainly as an inexpensive filler in soap
making, canola or rapeseed oil does tend to
produce a soft, low-lathering soap and is best
used in combination with an equal or higher
percentage of coconut oil.

INCI: *Canola* for canola oil or *Brassica campestris* for
rapeseed oil
Oleic: 32%
Linoleic: 15%
Palmitic: 1%
Iodine: 105–120

CASTOR SEED OIL *

Used in soap for its high foaming properties,
this oil is particularly useful in shampoos and
shaving soaps but does accelerate trace.

INCI: *Ricinus communis*
Ricinoleic: 90%
Linoleic: 3–4%
Oleic: 3–4%
Iodine: 82–90

COCOA BUTTER

High in saturated fats and vitamin E, cocoa
butter is a natural moisturizer that will add
hardness to your soap and body to your creams.

INCI: *Theobroma cacao*
Oleic: 34–36%
Stearic: 31–35%
Palmitic: 25–30%
Linoleic: 3%
Iodine: 33–42

COCONUT OIL *

Copra and RBD (refined, bleached and
deodorized) coconut oil are the soap maker's
staple, creating a hard bar soap with a rich foam.
Used alone it can be drying so should be combined
with other oils. The rarer virgin coconut oil is
high in saturated fatty acids and acts as a good
moisturizer and thickener in creams.

INCI: *Cocos nucifera*
Lauric: 39–54%
Myristic: 15–23%
Palmitic: 6–11%
Oleic: 4–11%
Stearic: 1–4%
Linoleic: 1–2%
Iodine: <10

COMFREY OIL

Macerated in sunflower or olive oil, comfrey
contains allantoin, a cell-proliferant that helps
repair damaged tissue.

INCI: *Symphytum officianale*
The fatty acid profile for comfrey oil depends on
the base oil it is macerated in. Clarify this with
your supplier.

EMU OIL

This is an anti-inflammatory oil popular with
Australian and South African soap makers,
and is becoming more so in the US. Whilst I
personally can't bring myself to try soap made
from emus, reports are that it adds greatly to
the moisturizing qualities of bar soap.

INCI: *Emu oil*
Linoleic: 14%
Myristic: 0.4%
Oleic: 50%
Palmitic: 21%

Stearic: 9%

Iodine: 75

EVENING PRIMROSE OIL

High in gamma linolenic acid, excellent in creams and lotions for mature skin.

INCI: *Oenothera biennis*

Palmitic: 5.5–7%

Oleic: 5–11%

Stearic: 1.5–2.5%

Linoleic: 70–77%

Iodine: 135–165

GRAPE SEED OIL

A light base oil that is easily absorbed by the skin, firms up and regenerates. Rich in vitamins and minerals.

INCI: *Vitis vinifera*

Linoleic: 58–78%

Oleic: 12–28%

Palmitic: 5–11%

Stearic: 3–6%

Iodine: 125–142

HEMP SEED OIL *

High percentage of essential fatty acids and vitamins, moisturizing and helps to balance dry skin. Makes a gorgeous soap but used on its own has a short shelf life.

INCI: *Cannabis sativa*

Oleic: 12%

Linoleic: 57%

Palmitic: 6%

Stearic: 2%

Linolenic: 21%

Iodine: 166.5

JOJOBA OIL

Actually a wax, not an oil, jojoba easily penetrates the skin and provides a protective barrier. Adds thickness to creams and is very conditioning when used in hair products.

INCI: *simmondsia chinensis*

Oleic: 10–13%

Iodine: 80–85

LARD (pig fat) *
Makes a hard, cleansing soap bar with plenty of foam.
INCI in soap: *sodium lardate*
Oleic: 46%
Palmitic: 28%
Stearic: 13%
Linoleic: 6%
Myristic: 1%
Iodine: 43–45

MACADAMIA NUT OIL
High in omega 9, this fatty oil penetrates and moisturizes dry and mature skin.
INCI: *macademia tetraphylla*
Oleic: 54–63%
Palmitic: 7–10%
Stearic: 2–6%
Linoleic: 1–3%
Iodine: 73–79

MARULA OIL
Great antioxidant, originally used on its own as a cleansing, moisturizing body oil.
INCI: *sclerocarya birrea*
Oleic: 70–78%
Palmitic: 9–12%
Stearic: 5–8%
Linoleic: 4–7%
Iodine: 70–76

MEADOWFOAM OIL
A very stable oil that is great for dry or sensitive skin. Highly moisturizing and rejuvenating, it is great in creams and lotions.
INCI: *Limnanthes alba*
Oleic: 3.2%
Iodine: 92

MELON OIL (Kalahari)
Rich in fatty acids and vitamin C, detoxifying and rejuvenating. Light and easily absorbed by the skin.
INCI: *Citrallus lanatus*
Oleic: 16–17%
Palmitic: 11–12%

Stearic: 7.5–8%
Linoleic: 50–70%
Iodine: 120–130

OLIVE OIL *
The first choice of many soap makers, pure olive oil soaps get better as they get older but trace and harden very slowly. You either love or hate the slightly oily feel and the slow lather. A relatively low cost option for a cream or lotion base.
INCI: *Olea Europaea*
Oleic: 63–81%
Palmitic: 7–14%
Linoleic: 5–15%
Stearic: 3–5%
Iodine: 79–95

PALM OIL *
Provided this is purchased from an ecologically-sound source it is a staple oil for soap makers providing an inexpensive, hard, long lasting soap bar with a relatively low foam. Palm oil is produced from the fleshy fruit of the palm.
INCI in soap: *Elaeis Guineensis*
Palmitic: 43–45%
Oleic: 38–40%
Linoleic: 9–11%
Stearic: 4–5%
Iodine: 45–57

PALM KERNEL OIL *
Widely used as a base in industrial soap production, this is a good bulking oil and has a different fatty acid make up from palm oil. Because of the high lauric content this oil traces very quickly. Palm kernel oil is produced from the kernel of the palm fruit
INCI: *Elaeis guineensis*
Lauric: 47%
Oleic: 18%
Myristic: 14%
Palmitic: 9%
Iodine: 37

PEACH KERNEL OIL

High in protein, vitamins A and E and omega 6. Good for all skin types and lovely in creams.

INCI: *Prunus persica*

Oleic: 55–75%

Palmitic: 5–8%

Linoleic: 15–35%

Iodine: 108–118

ROSEHIP SEED OIL

Rich in vitamins A and C, this cell regenerator is great for stretch marks and scar tissue.

INCI: *Rosa mosqueta*

Palmitic: 3-5%

Oleic: 10–20%

Linoleic: 26–37%

Stearic: 1–3%

Iodine: 179–192

SEA BUCKTHORN OIL

High in vitamin C and B-carotene, natural antioxidant known to combat wrinkles, eczema and dry skin.

INCI: *Hippophae rhamnoides*

Palmitic: 34-35%

Linoleic: 35–36%

Iodine: 86

SUNFLOWER OIL *

High in fatty acids and easily absorbed by the skin, a good base oil for all skin types. Great option for liquid soap and as a bulk oil in bar soaps although, it should be combined with coconut oil or the soap will be very soft.

INCI: (*Helianthus anuus*)

Linoleic: 70%

Oleic: 16%

Palmitic: 7%

Stearic: 4%

Iodine: 119–138

SHEA BUTTER (KARITE)

High in saturated fats, an effective moisturizer that stimulates cell growth, good for stretch marks and scar tissue. Great moisturizer and hardener

when used in bar soaps. Thickens creams.

INCI: *Butyrospermum parkii*

Oleic: 40–55%

Stearic: 35–45%

Linoleic: 3–8%

Palmitic: 3–7%

Iodine: 55–71

TALLOW (beef fat) *

A traditional soap making ingredient that produces a hard, conditioning soap bar.

INCI in soap: *Sodium tallowate*

Oleic: 37–43%

Palmitic: 24–32%

Stearic: 20–25%

Myristic: 3–6%

Linoleic: 2–3%

Iodine: 43–45

WHEATGERM OIL

An anti-bacterial that stimulates skin cells. High in vitamins and essential fatty acids but goes rancid very quickly.

INCI: *Triticum vulgare*

Linoleic: 55–60%

Oleic: 13–21%

Palmitic: 13–20%

Stearic: 2%

Iodine: 125–135

VITAMIN E OIL

A natural antioxidant that will extend the life of your products. Smooths dry and rough skin.

INCI: *Tocopheryl*

SCENTS AND SENSIBILITIES

One of the most important elements of your soap is fragrance. Those of us who want our products to be totally natural opt for essential oils diffused or pressed from plants or citrus fruits, used both for their fragrance and for their therapeutic value. The second option is synthetic fragrance oils. These can imitate scents that would be too expensive to achieve naturally (such as rose), and they can also mimic fruit and even lemon meringue pie if that is the perfume you are trying to achieve. Whatever your preference, the one important fact you need to bear in mind if you are planning on marketing your soap is 'no smell, no sell'.

In mass produced soap, fragrance is added well after the chemical reaction is complete and it is therefore stable and strong in the soap. In cold processed soap making we add the fragrance while the chemical reaction is going on and therefore we have to be careful that the blend of oils we choose will withstand this saponification process. The extensive art of aromatherapy would fill this book all on its own but basically, essential oils are split into three categories or 'notes', being top, middle and base notes. A 'top note' fragrance is the first to reach your nose but can be fleeting, a 'middle note' is the core of the fragrance blend whilst a 'base note' anchors the blend and gives it a sensuous undertone. When composing a blend for a cold process soap it helps considerably if you use a combination of the three notes, or at very least include a base note oil.

Another useful trick is to add your essential oil to dry matter before you put it in your soap. If you plan to put herbs, petals or clays in your soap, pour the essential oils over them first — this process helps to suspend the fragrance in the soap mix and increases its holding power. When working with liquid soap you don't have this problem as the saponification is complete before you add the fragrance.

When buying essential oils, always go to a reputable supplier and ensure that the oils are

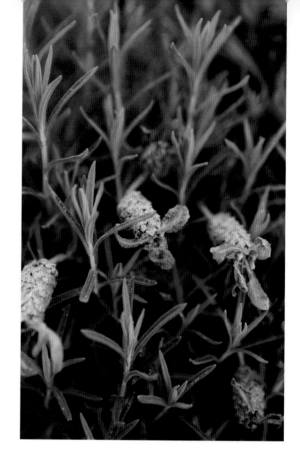

100 per cent pure. This does not mean you have to use the most expensive varieties, but do check that oils do not contain dilutants as these may interfere with the saponification process and cause your soap mixture to seize. Likewise, when using artificial fragrances only buy from a supplier who understands cold process soap making and make sure the fragrances are of a cosmetic grade and not just produced for fragrancing a room or for candle making.

If you are making toiletries for yourself, perhaps because you have allergies or sensitive skin, you must bear in mind that both natural and unnatural fragrances can be very high in allergens and these, along with pigments, are the biggest cause of skin irritation. In Europe, by law your fragrance content must not be more than 2 per cent of your total soap formula, and this is for good reason. Essential oils are extremely concentrated and powerful and, whilst when used with knowledge and care they are undoubtedly beneficial to the skin, if you use them heavily just to increase fragrance they can be dangerous. EU cosmetic legislation now also requires you to list on your product labels some specific allergens that occur naturally within many essential oils.

When making creams and lotions you can create a light scent by replacing the water content with a flower water or hydrosol (see page 125). Because only a tiny amount of essential oil is needed to fragrance a cream, you can also use some of the precious essential oils such as neroli or Roman chamomile, both of which are reasonably safe for those prone to eczema or dermatitis. Below are some of the more popular essential oils and their properties. You will also find a chart on pages 110–111 that will help you choose fragrances for specific skin types.

CARDAMOM (*Elletaria cardamomum*) Top note
Extracted from the plant seed, this pungent and spicy oil works well with blends of cinnamon, orange and frankincense. Irritant, so use only in very small quantities.

CEDARWOOD ATLAS (*Cedrus atlantica*) Base note
Distilled from the wood this refreshing, clean fragrance is great for masculine toiletries and holds up well in cold process soap.

CHAMOMILE (Roman) (*Athemis nobilis*) Top note
Distilled from the flowers and leaves, a great choice for those with sensitive skin, including babies.

CINNAMON LEAF (*Cinnamomum verum J.*) Middle note
Not to be confused with cinnamon bark oil (which should not be used), cinnamon leaf oil is fine in small quantities and blends beautifully with ginger and orange.

CLOVE (*Eugenia caryophyllata – bud*) Base/middle note
Useful boost for spicy blends but should be used in tiny quantities as it is high in allergens. Should not be used during pregnancy. Accelerates trace in soaps.

EUCALYPTUS (*Eucalyptus globulus*) Top note
Powerful clean scent, good for blending with citrus fragrances, antifungal and antiseptic.

FRANKINCENSE (*Boswellia carterii*) Base note
Distilled gum resin and precious oil with a deep, spicy, sweet fragrance. Blend with lavender and neroli for a real treat.

GERANIUM (*Pelargonium graveolens*) Middle note
The Egyptian variety is reasonably priced and holds well in soap. This is the closest you will get to a rose scent without breaking the bank. Delicious heady, floral fragrance.

GINGER (*Zingiber officinale*) Middle note
Adds an interesting twist to citrus blends but can cause irritation so only use in very small amounts.

GRAPEFRUIT (*Citrus paradisi*) Top note
Does not hold well in cold processed soaps but a good choice for liquid soap. Nice addition to lavender.

HOWOOD LEAF (*Cinnamomum camphora*) Middle note
Only use in very small quantities due to the possibility of skin irritation. Has a sweet, earthy fragrance that blends well with sweet orange and lavender.

LAVENDER (*Lavendula officinalis*) Top note
A wonderful staple oil that holds up well. Even if you hate lavender, understand that lavender soap outsells all other varieties 8 to 1.

LEMON (*Citrus limonum*) Top note
Therapeutic and healing when used in creams, but unless cleverly blended does not hold up well in cold processed soap. Try Litsea cubeba or Lemongrass as a refreshing citrus alternative .

LEMONGRASS (*Cymbopogon citratus*) Top note
Refreshing citrus fragrance that holds well in cold processed soap and blends well with lavender. Excellent choice for men but can cause irritation so keep the percentages low.

MANDARIN (*Citrus reticulate*) Top note
A citrus scent with floral undertones, lovely in liquid soap and creams but no staying power in cold processed soaps.

MAY CHANG (*Litsea cubeba*) Top note
Has a great citrus scent that can be used to anchor other scents. Holds up very well in cold process soap.

NEROLI (*Melaleuca viridiflora*) Middle note
Used as the basis for *eau de cologne*, this bitter orange blossom scent is highly prized and priced so should not be wasted in cold processed soap.

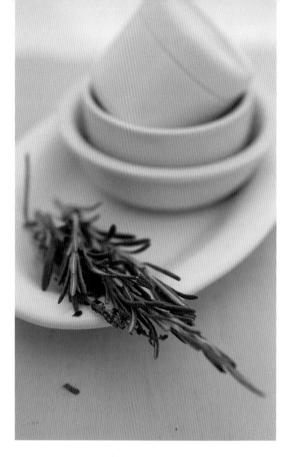

HERBS, SPICES AND ADDITIVES

Once you have decided on the oils you want to use in your base recipe there are numerous delights you can add at the trace stage (when your soap thickens) to enhance the texture and performance of your product. This is the really fun part of soap making.

If you want a bar to have exfoliating qualities experiment by adding dried herbs, poppy seeds, pumice powder, ground orange or lemon peel, dried seaweed, oatmeal, bran (or other pulses), salt or sugar. There are also a vast number of seeds and fruit powders on the market such as raspberry and strawberry seeds and ground fruit kernels (try olive or apricot for a scrubby effect).

Dried flower petals (rose, lavender and calendula) can also be added at trace but bear in mind that only calendula (marigold) will retain its colour – sadly everything else turns brown over time.

The amount of dried additive you use is purely a matter of taste and has no bearing on the saponification process, but if you are using any dried 'live matter' it is a good idea to add 1 per cent vitamin E oil to your formula to help preserve it.

Pureed fruit or aloe vera can also be added to your soap. Deduct the weight from the weight of the water in your formula and add the pulp/gel to the lye water before mixing the soap.

Argile clay, added at trace, gives your soap 'slip' and helps to draw out any impurities in the skin. It can also be used in creams and is available in green, pink, yellow and red so it adds natural colour (see page 59). Coffee grounds act as deodorizers and are a good option for kitchen soap as they will help to get the smell of garlic and onions off your hands. Simply make a pot of coffee, drain out the coffee grounds and add these at trace. If you want a dark brown soap, use actual coffee instead of water to make up your lye.

For a harder soap try adding up to 2 per cent beeswax to your formula. Beeswax is also a useful emulsifier and thickener for creams

PALMAROSA (*Cymbopogon martini*) Middle note
Fresh, sweet and floral with a rose geranium overtone. Has moisturizing and balancing properties.

PATCHOULI (*Pogostemon patchouli*) Base note
The stuff of incense sticks and cachous, patchouli is a wonderful anchor for blends and brings on waves of 60s nostalgia when used on its own. Lovely with geranium and/or lavender.

PEPPERMINT (*Metha piperata*) Top note
A stimulating oil that is good in foot creams and insect repellents. Should not be used during the first three months of pregnancy.

TEA TREE (*Melaleuca alternifolia*) Top note
Antiseptic in both purpose and fragrance and will help to preserve creams and lotions. Good for insect bites and acne.

YLANG YLANG (*Cananga odorata*) Middle note
Heady floral fragrance that holds up well in cold process soap and adds a touch of romance to a blend of oils.

and is particularly good in pure olive oil soaps. Honey is a scrumptious additive and is used for its emollient qualities. It can be added at trace if warmed slightly before use or alternatively add it to your lye solution.

COLOURINGS

The earth provides us with a number of natural ingredients that can be used to colour soaps and creams. The following natural ingredients are particularly useful for muted colours. Dilute the colourings in a drop of warm water and then mix with a spoonful or two of your traced soap before adding this back to your main batch and mixing thoroughly. This will avoid a speckled effect.

CARROT POWDER	ORANGE
CAYENNE PEPPER	SALMON
COCOA POWDER	BROWN
COFFEE	BROWN
CURRY POWDER	YELLOW TO PEACH
GINGER POWDER	PEACH
MADDER	PINK
PAPRIKA	PEACH
SPIRULINA	GREEN
TURMERIC	CORAL

Two very useful gifts from nature are alkanet, which is a tree bark, and the seed annatto, commonly used to colour cheese. Both of these should be infused in warm sunflower or olive oil before use. Simply heat a cupful of oil and add 1/3 of a cupful of bark or seeds and leave this to infuse until it is deep purple, or yellow in the case of annatto. Alkanet will turn your soap anything from grey to a rosy lavender depending on the alkalinity of the soap whilst annatto gives you a warm sunshine yellow.

If you want to achieve bright colours there is no choice but to use cosmetic grade oxide powders or FD&C or D&C (food drug and cosmetic) grade manmade pigments. Oxides are sometimes sold as 'natural' but in reality they are an inorganic compound made up from synthetically prepared iron oxides that include some hydrated form of naturally occurring mineral deposits.

FD&C and D&C colourants are manmade but very tiny amounts are needed to colour your products. For this reason they are considered entirely safe.

When using oxides, dissolve approximately 3/4 tsp in 28 g (1 oz) of warm distilled water – this is sufficient for a 1 kg (2 lb) batch of soap. When using FD&C and D&C colourants you need only enough pigment to cover the tip of a teaspoon dissolved in the same amount of water to produce quite a strong colour. Add these colours drop by drop at trace until you achieve the shade you want. For liquid soap and creams you can use liquid food colourants but be aware that only one drop of colourant will give you quite a strong colour.

Bar Soaps

THE BASICS

THE SIMPLEST AND MOST ENERGY efficient way to make soap is the cold process method. The equipment needed is very basic and you can make soap pretty much anywhere you have access to water. Previously I have used a method requiring access to a heat source but in this book nearly all the soaps have been made by chopping cold fats into very small pieces, adding any oils the recipe requires and then pouring the freshly made lye solution directly onto the cold fats and oils. No heat source or thermometers are required. This is a huge time and energy saver that does not in any way diminish the quality of the finished soap.

If you prefer to melt your fats and oils over a heat source before adding your lye solution, wait until both the oils and the lye reach a similar temperature. Pouring boiling hot lye over slightly warmed oils can cause overheating and in some instances this can result in the mixture boiling-up and overflowing (a bit like a volcano).

Traditional soap makers in France use a hot process method, boiling the oils and lye together for several weeks before salting off the soap from the solution. There are more kitchen-friendly methods of hot processing your soap and I have used these in two recipes on pages 60 and 63. One advantage of hot process soap is that the chemical reaction is complete once the soap is poured into moulds, so it is immediately safe to use. Whilst some curing time is still needed to allow the moisture in the soap to evaporate, this is not as lengthy as the curing time required in the cold process method.

Another soap making method is 'melt and pour'. Whilst this method can produce colourful and very artistic clear bar soaps, you have no control over your base ingredients as you simply buy a ready-made soap compound, melt it down, add colour and fragrance and pour into moulds. As this book is about making products from scratch I haven't included any 'melt and pour' recipes.

EQUIPMENT

When I first set-up my business we somehow managed to make soap using plastic buckets, a hand-held electric drill and some large wooden boxes for moulds. This is what makes soap making an industry that can be created in any outreach in the world. Here is what you will need for cold processed soap making:

Plastic buckets x 2
These will be used to mix-up your lye solution and your soap. Domestic buckets are fine but if you are buying new ones buy rubbery rather than light-weight plastic as they will last longer.

Electric stick blender
This speeds up the stirring process enormously. For large batches use an electric drill with a stainless steel or stripped metal paint stirrer attachment.

Plastic, polythene or glass measuring jugs
Buy half a dozen of these as you will find a million uses for them.

Stainless steel spoon
Large with a long handle.

Moulds and greaseproof paper
Read more in the mould section on page 22.

Knife
Large, non-serrated and straight edged for cutting fats and finished soaps.

Rubber gloves
To protect your hands when handling sodium hydroxide and fresh soap.

Eye protection

Perspex glasses or plastic goggles available from DIY shops.

Sponges, kitchen roll and dishcloths
For cleaning-up during and afterwards.

Kitchen scales
Digital scales weighing in very small increments. You need specialist scales if you are making soap to sell.

Plastic beakers
For diluting colourants and weighing additives.

Droppers
Plastic or glass for adding colourants and essential oils.

Measuring spoons
For measuring out ingredients.

Kebab skewers, knitting needles or a fork
For making swirls in your soap.

Plastic spatulas
For scraping the soap out of the bucket.

Sodium hydroxide (caustic soda/lye/NaOH)
Available in the plumbing section of DIY shops. This needs to be at least 95 per cent pure.

Distilled or Spring water
For mixing the lye.

Vinegar
If you splash yourself with lye, this will neutralize it.

Plastic wrap
For covering your freshly made soap.

Sugar thermometers x 2
Most of the recipes in this book use the very cold process method and do not require these but traditionally you should measure the temperature of your oils and diluted lye and mix them together only when they reach the same temperature.

For hot processed soap and for liquid soap making you will also need a stainless steel stock pot and a larger pot to stand this in to create a bain marie or double boiler. In addition you will need a heat source hot enough to keep your soap at a rolling boil.

> **NOTE** All pots and utensils that will come in contact with your soap must be made from stainless steel or plastic. Aluminium can react with the lye and flake off into your soap. You can use enamel but only if there are no chips on it. Avoid pots with a non-stick finish.

MOULDS

In theory you can use any wooden, plastic, rubber or cardboard container as a mould for your cold or hot processed soap, as long as it will not leak. If it is inflexible you must line the mould with baking parchment or plastic wrap so you can release your soap easily when it is set.

In practice the speed of the saponification process and the quality of your finished soap can be influenced by the size of your mould – the larger the mould/soap batch, the greater the heat generated by the process. Block, tray or loaf moulds will give a more even soap than individual moulds.

If you are making soap as a hobby, silicone baking moulds are brilliant as the soap does not stick to the surface so you do not have to line your mould. You can also use cylindrical crisp containers, flexible food storage containers and even lengths of drainpipe to create curved shaped soaps (these should be greased with coconut oil or cooking spray before use).

If you are planning to sell your soap there are a number of professional moulds available that are sold with cutting devices to make it easy for you to ensure that each soap you make is the same size and weight. These moulds are made either from wood or HDPE (high-density polyethylene) – a heat-resistant plastic that is easy to clean. You can also buy HDPE slab moulds which have plastic strips that divide the soap into equal-sized bars (as does the famous 'Nizzy' mould which Australian soap makers swear by).

You should ensure that any mould you use is flexible. Clear rigid plastic shapes are great for melt and pour soaps but cold process soap does tend to get stuck to the bottom and you may end up having to break the mould to get your soap out. Before resorting to this try putting your soap-filled mould into the freezer for half an hour, as this can help to release it.

NOTE The recipes in this book are all designed to fit a 1½ kg (3 lb) mould.

SAFE SOAP

Both bar and liquid soaps are made with sodium hydroxide (caustic soda, lye) which, without careful and sensible handling, can give you a nasty burn. If you take note of the following, all will be well:

• Store sodium hydroxide in an airtight and childproof container and mark it 'poison'.

• Work in a well ventilated space and mix lye outside if possible.

• Wear rubber gloves when handling lye or fresh soap.

• Always add lye to the water and not the other way around (think 'LTW' – lye to water). If you pour water into your lye it can bubble-up and burn you.

• Wear a dust mask over your mouth and nose when adding the lye to the water (you only need wear this for about two minutes whilst you stir the solution).

• Always wear eye goggles or protective glasses when handling lye and mixing your soap.

• When pouring dry lye into the water in the open air hold the lye container inside and below the top edge of the bucket or a gust of wind can send it flying in all directions.

• Do not leave soap or your lye mix unattended or in the reach of children or pets.

• When making soap keep a bottle of vinegar nearby. If you splash yourself with lye, rinse quickly with cold water and then apply the vinegar, which will help to neutralize the lye.

• Turn off your phone when mixing lye and weighing ingredients - you really must give it your full attention.

• Make sure your stick blender is immersed in your soap before you turn it on.

• When cleaning your soap bucket, first wipe it with paper then put the paper in a sealed bag in with your garbage. Wash all your utensils with regular washing up liquid after wiping the residue off with paper. (Fresh soap contains a lot of oil, and if you pour this down your sink on a cold day it can solidify and block your drains.)

• Do not wear jewellery or keep a pin board or any small objects near your soap making area to avoid them falling into your soap.

• Cover your hair to avoid getting any in the soap.

SAPONIFICATION, SUPERFATTING AND ESSENTIAL STUFF

SAPONIFICATION IS WHAT HAPPENS WHEN you mix oils or fats with lye. Every botanical or animal oil or fat has its own unique saponification (or 'SAP') value, and this value determines exactly how much sodium hydroxide is required to turn that particular oil into soap. Getting this right is the most important factor in all methods of soap making and is the difference between producing a harsh, potentially caustic bar of soap and a gentle moisturizing bar.

On the chart opposite you will see a list of oils and two columns of numbers. The first column gives the SAP value for NaOH (sodium hydroxide) that should be used when making bar soaps. The second column gives the SAP value for KOH (potassium hydroxide) and should be used when making liquid soaps. The calculation is very simple – multiply the quantity of oil or fat you want to use (in grams) by its SAP value to give you the quantity of lye needed to turn it into soap.

For example to make soap using 500 g of coconut oil, multiply the NaOH SAP value for coconut oil (0.185) by 500 (0.185 x 500 = 92.5). This will tell you that you need 92 g of caustic soda to turn 500 g of coconut oil into soap (round any fractions up or down to the nearest whole number). For liquid soap do exactly as above but use the SAP value for KOH. If your recipe has several different oils or fats in it, calculate each one separately and then total the caustic soda up at the end. There are numerous online saponification programmes that will do this for you (see Resources on page 143).

SUPERFATTING

Once you have calculated the amount of caustic needed you can ensure that the soap will be gentle by superfatting it, or applying a 'lye discount'. Both of these terms mean exactly the same thing: either adding up to 5 per cent extra oils or reducing the amount of lye by up to 5 per cent. Deciding on what percentage is a little more complex, as it is determined by the stability of your oils. If you are using an oil with a tendency to go rancid quickly, only superfat by up to 2 per cent. If you want your soap to be extra oily or creamy, go up to 5 per cent. This comes with experience but for now, if you want to superfat a soap by say 3 per cent (which is fine for most formulas) do your basic calculations to establish how much lye is needed and then deduct 3 per cent from that amount.

When I first started soap making I learned to add between 2 and 5 per cent of a precious oil to use as a superfatter at the trace stage. Over the years the logic of this has made less and less sense to me. Think about it; your soap takes up to six weeks to fully saponify – how do the soap fairies know which oil in the batch they should leave unsaponified? For many years now I have been putting all of the oils together in the soap pot (including my superfatting oil), calculating the lye and deducting the superfat percentage and then adding the lye to the oils makes absolutely no difference the quality of my finished soaps, and so this is the method I now recommend using.

WATER CONTENT

The amount of water used in a formula is widely disputed amongst soap makers, but I have found that using 33 per cent of the total weight of the oils works best as it provides an even mix and gives me time to add my colours, herbs and essential oils without panicking. Remember to always use distilled or spring water when making soap.

SAPONIFICATION CHART

OILS AND FATS	SAP NaOH	SAP KOH	OILS AND FATS	SAP NaOH	SAP KOH
Almond	0.136	0.191	Lecithin	0.086	0.121
Apricot Kernel	0.135	0.189	Macadamia	0.139	0.195
Avocado	0.133	0.187	Maize (corn)	0.136	0.191
Babassu	0.175	0,245	Mango butter	0.134	0.188
Baobab	0.142	0.245	Meadowfoam	0.121	0.170
Bay berry (Laurel)	0.141	0.180	Neem	0.139	0.195
Beeswax	0.069	0.097	Niger seed	0.136	0.191
Borage / Starflower	0.136	0.191	Nutmeg butter	0.180	0.252
Brazil nut	0.175	0.245	Olive	0.134	0.188
Camelia/teaseed	0.136	0.191	Palm	0.141	0.198
Candelilla	0.042	0.059	Palm kernel	0.164	0.230
Canola (Rapeseed)	0.124	0.174	Peach kernel	0.137	0.192
Carnauba wax	0.057	0.080	Peanut (Groundnut)	0.136	0.191
Castor	0.129	0.181	Pecan	0.135	0.189
Cocoa butter	0.137	0.192	Poppyseed	0.138	0.194
Coconut	0.185	0.260	Pumpkinseed	0.134	0.188
Cod-liver oil	0.130	0.182	Pura	0.136	0.191
Corn (Maize)	0.136	0.191	Rapeseed (Canola)	0.124	0.174
Cottonseed	0.134	0.188	Ricebran oil	0.128	0.180
Emu	0.137	0.192	Rosa mosqueta/rosehip	0.138	0.194
Evening primrose	0.136	0.191	Safflower	0.136	0.191
Fish oils	0.133	0.187	Sesame seed	0.133	0.187
Flax	0.136	0.191	Shortening	0.138	0.194
Goose fat	0.137	0.192	Shea butter (Karite)	0.128	0.180
Grapeseed	0.127	0.178	Soybean (Soya)	0.135	0.189
Groundnut (peanut)	0.136	0.191	Stearic acid	0.143	0.200
Hazelnut	0.136	0.191	Sunflower	0.134	0.188
Hemp seed	0.135	0.189	Talllow – bear	0.139	0.195
Mafura Butter	0.200	0.194	Tallow, beef	0.140	0.196
Jojoba	0.068	0.095	Tallow, goat,sheep,deer	0.140	0.196
Marula Oil	0.135	0.189	Walnut	0.135	0.189
Lanolin	0.074	0.104	Watermelon (Kalahari)	0.133	0.187
Lard	0.138	0.194	Wheatgerm	0.131	0.180

CURING

When making cold processed soaps the saponification process can take up to six weeks to complete. In addition to this, to create a hard, long lasting soap bar, the water used in the process needs time to evaporate, and so soaps need to be cured. To do this, lay your cut bars on a tray with spaces in between so the air can circulate. Place them somewhere dry (an airing cupboard is ideal) and leave them for six weeks, turning them from time to time. If you use your soap before the curing process is complete it could irritate or sting your skin. How do I know when it's ready? The traditional method used by soap makers is 'the tongue test': wet your finger and rub it on the surface of your soap and then put that finger to your tongue. If it 'bites' or 'tingles' your soap needs longer to cure. If it just tastes like soap, it's ready. Once you have made a few batches of soap you will know from the hardness of the bar when the soap is ready.

Soap made using the hot process method does not need time to cure but it does need time for the water to evaporate. Likewise, liquid soaps are ready for use once the paste is diluted. The curing process can be reduced by half if you put your soaps in an enclosed space and keep a dehumidifier running 24/7. You do not need to cure your liquid soaps.

CUTTING YOUR SOAP

Soap can be cut into blocks using any straight edged blade or cheese wire, but if you are selling your soap it is important, for legal reasons, to ensure that the bars are all the same weight. There are simple devices available to cut your soap, or you can make something similar to a mitre block with a straight slit in it that enables you to slide your soap block forward to the same position each time before cutting a chunk off. When the soap should be cut depends to some degree on whether you have used soft or hard oils in your formula, but it is normally between 24 and 48 hours after it comes out the mould, by which time it should look and feel like hard

cheese. Be careful though as if you leave it too long the soap can become too hard to cut without crumbling.

INSULATING, GELLING AND TROUBLESHOOTING

'Gelling' is a phase that an oil and lye combination sometimes goes through during the saponification process. A dark shadow will appear at the centre of your soap and over a period of hours this shadow will spread out to the edges of your mould and then (usually over the next 24 hours) disappear. I say 'sometimes' because the question of whether a soap will gel or not depends on the recipe formula, the water content, the size and shape of the mould and the weather or ambient temperature you are working in (the warmer the environment and the larger the batch, the more likely your soap is to gel). Basically what happens during this phase is that the saponification process speeds up.

There is much debate as to whether a gelled soap is superior to an ungelled soap (i.e. one that has saponified more slowly). Many soap makers insulate their moulds by wrapping blankets round them in an attempt to achieve gel, others put their freshly poured soaps in the fridge hoping to avoid it. On the plus side, gelling usually produces a very hard bar of soap that cures relatively quickly, but on the minus side quite often the shadow on the surface of the soap results in permanent patches of uneven colour.

The most important thing to note is that if you attempt to cut your soap whilst it is in the gel phase, you will find yourself faced with a glutinous mess. So if a shadow appears on the surface of your soap make sure it has faded away before you attempt any cutting.

Natural soap making is alchemy, and as such we have to take into account some of the vagaries of nature. As an inexperienced soap maker working with the dreaded caustic soda, you may look at your finished soaps and be thrown into long, nail-biting sessions whilst you decide whether they are safe to use. Here are some of the most common soap ailments and their most likely causes, but be aware that most mistakes only happen if you have failed to calculate your basic formula correctly.

Crumbly soap

Caused by too little water or excess lye. Grate this up and use it as a laundry soap.

Curdling

Nearly always happens with goat's milk soap and with liquid soaps, especially when using two different lyes. Just keep stirring, it will be alright.

Mottled soap

Often occurs in soaps coloured with spices that haven't been stirred well enough but fine to use.

No Trace

Soaps made without lauric (palm/coconut) fats can take much longer to trace. If you are sure your basic formula has the correct amount of lye just keep zapping with your hand blender.

Powdering

White powder on the top of your soap is actually soda ash — completely harmless but not very pretty. Scrape or wipe it off and next time be sure you cover the surface of your soap mould with plastic wrap to prevent this.

Seizing or separation

You add your fragrance and suddenly the soap goes into shock and becomes a lump (or several lumps) of fat floating in a sea of oil. This is most commonly caused by compounds in your fragrance or essential oils and you can stir the oils and fat together and scoop the lot into your mould. If the soap doesn't absorb the oil over time, throw it out because it is probably lye heavy.

Pockets of moisture

Bubbles on the surface of your soap filled with brown fluid. If you have honey in your recipe this is probably the culprit, if you don't then these are possibly pockets of lye and you should discard the soap.

Soft Soap

Soaps made with 100 per cent liquid oils can take several weeks to harden, but if this is a 100 per cent olive oil soap it's worth the wait. If this is a regular batch containing coconut oil you have weighed your lye incorrectly. The soap won't hurt you but it will go gloopy when wet.

Dreaded orange spot

A common soap making disease caused by oxidisation of your oils. The surface of your soap will be covered with small orangey brown spots or bruises. Whilst the soap is safe to use, throw it out as this condition will spread to neighbouring soaps.

BASIC SOAP METHOD

1. Chop up the fats, then weigh the fats and base oils one by one and put them together in a plastic bucket.

2. Weigh the water in the second bucket.

3. Wearing goggles and gloves weigh the sodium hydroxide in a jug.

4. Line or grease moulds.

5. Weigh additives, essential oils and colourants.

6. If using several essential oils blend these together and add any herbs or dried additives you may be using.

7. Wearing your gloves, goggles and mask go to a well-ventilated area and pour the sodium hydroxide into the water. Stir with a long handled, stainless steel spoon until dissolved. The chemical reaction will cause the solution to

1

8

10

9

12

heat up and you will see steam and fumes rising from the bucket.

8. Pour the hot lye directly over the cold oils and stir until the oils and fats have dissolved.

9. Zap the mixture with a stick blender until it traces (zap in short bursts so the motor doesn't burn out).

> **NOTE** 'Trace' is the point when soap dribbled from a spoon back onto the surface of your batch will form a line. In 'light trace' this is just distinguishable, 'medium' trace it is quite clear and 'heavy' trace it is prominent.

10. Add herbs and/or colourants and stir in thoroughly with a spoon.

11. Add your essential oils if they are not already combined with previous ingredients. Stir well.

12. Pour your soap into your prepared moulds.

13. Place plastic wrap directly on the surface of your soap and leave for 48 hours.

14. Turn the soap out of the mould and cut into bars using a sharp, straight edged knife, a cutting blade or cheese wire.

15. Place your soaps on a tray (leaving spaces in between) and put them in a dry place for six weeks.

16. Wash and enjoy!

PRESENTATION

With each of the recipes in this book I have given you suggestions for packaging. Soap is a truly versatile product that can be squished, moulded and cut into many forms and fantasies – the only limitation you have is your imagination. When you are trying to come up with new ideas the first thing you should do is stop thinking of a bar of soap as just square or oblong.

For starters, soap on a rope can be many things. All you need is an electric drill to make a clean hole through any bar and thread a cord through it. Knot it at the bottom to secure.

It is worth remembering that all but the most discerning customers buy firstly because of presentation, and secondly because of the quality of the product itself. Ironically, the simpler your packaging (think Chanel white boxes), the classier the positioning and the higher the price you can demand. When designing your soaps think of upmarket bathrooms and what will look good displayed in them. Almost 60 per cent of soaps sold in the gift market are never used — they just sit for years in the bathroom looking pretty.

PURPOSE

Whilst we think of soap primarily as a product to wash ourselves with, there are numerous other ways it can be packaged and sold. Heavily-scented natural soap will fragrance a room and will certainly fragrance clothes. You can capitalize on this by cutting your oddments into interesting shapes and packaging them as drawer fresheners, or you could tie a ribbon through them so they can be hung on clothes hangers. If you use insect repelling essential oils in your soaps (such as citronella, rosemary or lemongrass), the drawer fresheners will also repel insects and moths. Selling soap as clothes wash bypasses all the lengthy cosmetic legislation and is a great way to package up soap offcuts. Simply grate the soap and package it in a bag — this could be a plain paper sack with a scoop, or muslin bag that can just be thrown in the washing machine.

Soap can also be moulded or cut into cubes to form beads. It can be carved with a craft knife (the Japanese carve wonderful flowers from it) and it can even be cut into small tiles which can then be used to create mosaics. Wet soap is a gluey substance, if you score the back of the tiles and wet them you can press them onto paper and they will stick firmly to it.

DECORATION

Soap can be decorated in so many ways. The important thing is to forget that it is a bar of soap.

Items such as shells, seaweed, even money can be embedded in the top — wet the surface just after cutting and push them in. If you want to follow a popular trend and stud your soap with pink rosebuds it's a very good idea to dip the rosebuds in candlewax first. The problem with untreated botanicals is that when the soap gets wet they turn brown and soggy, and even a small amount of wetness may cause the flowers/plants to go mouldy. Pure food grade gold leaf can be pressed onto the surface of freshly cut soap to great effect and powdered mica (which does not hold up well when used as a colourant) will add a metallic or pearlized sheen when sprinkled on the top of a newly cut bar.

Paper decals can be embedded in the surface of a soap and you can even buy soap paints and stencil names or initials onto your bars. You can also achieve this by pouring fresh soap onto a stencil placed on a ready cut bar. Cake decorations (hundreds and thousands and silver balls) can be used to decorate your soaps, and silk flowers, millinery decorations and many items, perhaps originally bought for scrap booking, can be applied either to the soap itself or to your packaging.

If you are looking for an idea just go to your nearest shop and think soap!

PURE AND GENTLE

AN INCREASING NUMBER OF PEOPLE SEEM to be suffering from allergies and skin problems. While some people are quite plainly allergic to pure soap products they are vastly outnumbered by those who simply cannot tolerate synthetic detergent bars. The cold process soaps in this book contain pure glycerine which helps protect and moisturize the skin, but as fragrances (natural or otherwise) and colourants contribute greatly to skin problems you need to be extremely careful about what you add to your soaps (and creams) if you are trying to create a product for allergy prone skin.

While there are a limited number of essential oils that can be used in very small quantities in your pure and gentle soaps, it is best to keep soaps for allergy-prone skin as simple as possible. This section contains the best recipes I can come up with for those suffering from eczema and related problems. The soaps are packed with soothing ingredients and superfatted by 5 per cent to ensure no lye can survive.

Purity

This super mild soap is suitable for use on babies and on your face. It has no colour or fragrance and has shea butter for maximum moisturizing qualities. It is superfatted by 5 per cent and so includes vitamin E oil to help to preserve the free oils from rancidity.

INGREDIENTS

240 g (9½ oz) coconut oil

200 g (8 oz) shea butter

400 g (16 oz) sweet almond oil

100 g (4 oz) borage oil

50 g (2 oz) apricot kernel oil

327 g (13 oz) spring or distilled water

138 g (5½ oz) sodium hydroxide

10 ml (2 tsp) vitamin E oil

Superfatted at 5%

1 Weigh the coconut oil and shea butter, cut into small chunks and place in a plastic bucket. Weigh and add the almond, borage and apricot oils.

2 Put on your rubber gloves and goggles. Weigh the water in a plastic bucket. Weigh the sodium hydroxide in a jug.

3 In a well ventilated area and wearing gloves, mask and goggles, pour the sodium hydroxide into the water, stir with a long handled, stainless steel spoon until dissolved then set aside. Remove mask.

4 Pour the caustic solution into the oils. Stir manually until the fats and oils have dissolved and then bring the soap to a light trace using a stick blender.

5 Add the vitamin E oil. Mix in thoroughly with either a spoon or a blender and pour into a prepared 1½ kg (3 lb) mould.

6 Leave the soap to set for approximately 48 hours or until it has reached a 'hard cheese' consistency. Turn out of the mould and cut into bars. Cure the bars for four to six weeks before use.

VARIATION

For mature skin, deduct 1 tsp almond oil from your formula and replace this with 1 tsp evening primrose oil added at trace.

PACKAGING IDEA

For a perfect baby gift, package in a white box with a clear lid together with the Baby's Bottom Cream on page 117 and tie with a blue or pink ribbon.

Calendula and Goat's Milk

Goat's milk is a deceptive ingredient. It looks and smells horrid when you mix it with the lye but it makes a beautiful creamy soap that is very mild. I've added a dash of chamomile and lavender essential oils here as both are safe to use on sensitive skin.

1 Weigh the coconut oil and cocoa butter, chop into small chunks and put in a plastic bucket. Weigh and add the olive and avocado oils. Measure out the essential oils and blend them together.

2 Put on your rubber gloves and goggles. Weigh the water in a plastic bucket and the goat's milk in a jug and mix together in the bucket. Weigh the sodium hydroxide in a jug.

3 In a well ventilated area and wearing gloves, mask and goggles, pour the sodium hydroxide into the water and milk mixture and stir with a long handled, stainless steel spoon until dissolved. The goat's milk may curdle and turn yellow. It will also throw off fumes that smell of ammonia but continue stirring and keep your mask on. When the mixture is as even as you can get it, set aside. Remove mask.

4 Pour the caustic solution into the oils. Stir manually until the fats and oils have dissolved and then bring the soap to a light trace using a stick blender. Add the essential oil blend and stir thoroughly.

5 Sprinkle in the calendula petals — the amount you use is not critical, just enough to make the soap look pretty. Mix in thoroughly with a spoon and pour into a prepared 1½ kg (3 lb) mould.

6 Leave the soap to set for approximately 48 hours or until it has reached a 'hard cheese' consistency. Turn out of the mould and cut into bars. Cure the bars for four to six weeks before use.

INGREDIENTS

300 g (12 oz) coconut oil

50 g (2 oz) cocoa butter

600 g (24 oz) olive oil

50 g (2 oz) avocado oil

165 g (6 oz) spring or distilled water

165 g (6 oz) full fat goat's milk

142 g (5½ oz) sodium hydroxide

A handful of calendula petals

ESSENTIAL OILS

2.5 ml (½ tsp) Roman chamomile

2.5 ml (½ tsp) lavender

Superfatted at 5%

VARIATION

To create a soap with antiseptic properties replace the chamomile and lavender essential oils with a blend of tea tree and lemon essential oils.

PACKAGING IDEA

Cut the base of this soap with a wavy-edged herb cutter to help the soap to drain and stop it going gooey then tie it to a wooden soap dish with raffia.

Green Clay and Oatmeal

This gentle layered soap is great for exfoliating and the green clay will draw impurities from the skin. I've included a small percentage of castor oil here as it is a poweful antioxidant that conditions the skin, but be aware that soaps containing castor oil trace very quickly.

INGREDIENTS

400 g (16 oz) coconut oil

400 g (16 oz) olive oil

100 g (4 oz) castor oil

50 g (2 oz) rosehip seed oil

50 g (2 oz) sunflower oil

14 g (½ oz) green clay

14 g (½ oz) oatmeal

330 g (13 oz) spring or distilled water

146 g (5¾ oz) sodium hydroxide

ESSENTIAL OILS

2.5 ml (½ tsp) rose geranium

2.5 ml (½ tsp) lemon

Superfatted at 5%

1 Weigh the coconut oil, chop into small chunks and put in a plastic bucket. Weigh and add the olive, castor, rosehip seed and sunflower oils. Weigh the green clay and oatmeal.

2 Put on your rubber gloves and goggles. Weigh the water in a plastic bucket. Weigh the sodium hydroxide in a jug. Add just enough water from the weighed quantity to the green clay to make it fluid.

3 In a well ventilated area and wearing gloves, mask and goggles, pour the sodium hydroxide into the water, stir with a long handled, stainless steel spoon until dissolved then set aside. Remove mask.

4 Blend the essential oils together and pour half onto the oatmeal and the other half onto the green clay. Pour the caustic solution into the oils. Stir manually until the fats and oils have dissolved and then bring the soap to a light trace using a stick blender.

5 Divide the soap equally between two jugs. Add the green clay to one jug and the oatmeal to the other and stir thoroughly. Zap the soap containing the green clay with a blender until it is at heavy trace and pour it into the moulds (if using individual moulds pour to the halfway mark). Carefully pour the oatmeal soap over the top.

6 Leave the soap to set for approximately 48 hours or until it has reached a 'hard cheese' consistency. Turn out of the mould and cut into bars. Cure the bars for four to six weeks before use.

VARIATION

For a really scrubby foot soap, replace the oatmeal with coarse pumice powder, increasing the quantity so that the bottom layer is almost solid pumice.

PACKAGING IDEA

Plait several strands of raffia together to form two ropes. Stack three soaps together and tie the two raffia ropes round the soaps, knotting at the top.

FRUIT SOAPS

FRUIT FLAVOURED SOAPS SELL WELL, WHICH may be a problem for those of us who strive to keep our soaps entirely 'natural' as, with the exception of most of the citrus varieties, very few fruits are available as pure essential oils. If you want true fruit smells you have to resort to using artificial fragrance oils (there are some very good ones available designed specifically for cold process soap).

You can, of course, gain the unquestionable benefits of fruit (vitamins, omega acids etc.) by including fruit oils and extracts in your soap, but these will not give your soap fragrance or colour. There are also powdered fruit extracts on the market and you can use dried, powdered citrus peel, which is not only exfoliating but also bursts into numerous tiny yellow starlets that will decorate the surface of your soap.

Another option is to add liquidized fresh fruit to your soap, although lumps of fruit on the surface will attract bacteria so ensure that the mixture is completely lump free. When using fresh fruits you should always include an anti-oxidant such as vitamin E oil. Whilst you can add liquidized fruit at trace, to ensure a long shelf life add it to the lye and deduct from the weight of your water.

Fruit swirls

Swirled soaps are easier to achieve in a tray mould with a large surface area.
Swirling in small individual moulds can be very difficult
as the soap may go hard before you are half way through the batch.

INGREDIENTS

400 g (16 oz) coconut oil

300 g (12 oz) palm oil

300 g (12 oz) sunflower oil

330 g (13 oz) spring or
distilled water

148 g (6 oz) sodium hydroxide

15 ml (1 tbs) fruit fragrance oil

5 ml (1 tsp) diluted oxide

Superfatted at 3%

1 Weigh the coconut and palm oil, chop them into small chunks and put them a plastic bucket. Weigh and add the sunflower oil.

2 Put on your rubber gloves and goggles. Weigh the water in a plastic bucket. Weigh the sodium hydroxide in a jug.

3 In a well ventilated area and wearing gloves, mask and goggles, pour the sodium hydroxide into the water, stir with a long handled, stainless steel spoon until dissolved then set aside. Remove mask.

4 Pour the caustic solution into the oils. Stir manually until the fats and oils have dissolved and then bring the soap to a light trace using a stick blender.

5 Add the fragrance oils. Mix in thoroughly with either a spoon or blender. If you plan to use a fruit extract add it now.

6 Divide the batch into two jugs, ⅔ in one jug, ⅓ in the other. Pour the colourant into the jug containing the smaller batch of soap and mix thoroughly.

7 When the soap is at a heavy trace pour a layer of the uncoloured soap (approximately ⅓ of the jug) into the mould. Dribble lines of soap from the coloured batch over the surface. Trail your pointy object through the coloured soap to form the swirly pattern of your choice.

8 Repeat step 7 twice, building up layers of soap and swirling as you go until all your soap is in the mould. Tap the sides of the mould to level out the surface.

9 Leave the soap to set for approximately 48 hours or until it has reached a 'hard cheese' consistency. Turn out of the mould and cut into bars. Cure the bars for four to six weeks before use.

VARIATION

If you prefer to keep your soaps completely natural, use Annatto as a colourant instead of using the oxide. You can also replace the fragrance oil with 15 ml (1 tbs) lemon, grapefruit, sweet orange or mandarin essential oils to give you a pure, natural scent.

PACKAGING IDEA

Fruit soaps are great packed in little wooden crates filled with wood wool. You will find the crates in many craft outlets or just do a search on the internet for 'soap gift crates'.

Fig and Honey

Figs are one of the latest buzz ingredients to be included in soap and cosmetic ranges. They are packed with vitamin A and act as a humectant when combined with honey, attracting moisture to the skin. The seeds are also great natural exfoliants.

INGREDIENTS

500 g (20 oz) coconut oil

150 g (6 oz) shea butter

350 g (14 oz) olive oil

330 g (13 oz) spring or distilled water

154 g (6 oz) sodium hydroxide

2 medium fresh figs

15 ml (1 tbs) honey

5 ml (1 tsp) vitamin E oil

ESSENTIAL OILS

10 ml (2 tsp) ylang ylang

2.5 ml (½ tsp) cinnamon

2.5 ml (½ tsp) ginger

Superfatted at 3%

1 Weigh the coconut oil and shea butter, cut into small chunks and place in a plastic bucket. Weigh and add the olive oil.

2 Put on your rubber gloves and goggles. Weigh the water in a plastic bucket. Weigh the sodium hydroxide in a jug.

3 In a well ventilated area and wearing gloves, mask and goggles, pour the sodium hydroxide into the water, stir with a long handled, stainless steel spoon until dissolved then set aside. Remove mask.

4 Liquidize the figs using a stick blender, leaving no lumps. Pour the liquidized figs and honey into the caustic solution and stir until dissolved. Blend the essential oils together.

5 Pour the caustic solution into the oils. Stir manually until the fats and oils have dissolved and then bring the soap to a light trace using a stick blender. Add the vitamin E and essential oils. Combine thoroughly with either a spoon or your blender and pour into a prepared 1½ kg (3 lb) mould.

6 Leave the soap to set for approximately 48 hours or until it has reached a 'hard cheese' consistency. Turn out of the mould and cut into bars. Cure the bars for four to six weeks before use.

VARIATION

If you are using green figs, try adding a tablespoon of diluted green oxide at trace, and if you can't find fresh figs add 1 per cent fig extract at trace.

PACKAGING IDEA

If you are lucky enough to have access to fresh fig or vine leaves, package your soap in a parcel made from a fresh leaf and tie it up with raffia.

Apricot Skin Softener

Apricot kernel oil is rich in fatty acids and vitamin E (a natural anti-oxidant), and is easily absorbed by the skin. This is one of the key oils to use in soaps, creams and lotions for those with sensitive skin as it is deeply nourishing.

1 Weigh the coconut oil and shea butter, cut into small chunks and put in a plastic bucket. Weigh and add the olive, almond and apricot oils.

2 Put on your rubber gloves and goggles. Weigh the water in a plastic bucket. Weigh the sodium hydroxide in a jug.

3 In a well ventilated area and wearing gloves, mask and goggles, pour the sodium hydroxide into the water, stir with a long handled, stainless steel spoon until dissolved then set aside. Remove mask.

4 Blend the essential oils together and pour them onto the turmeric. Add enough water to make the consistency of a pourable paste.

5 Pour the caustic solution into the oils. Stir manually until the fats and oils have dissolved and then bring the soap to a light trace using a stick blender.

6 Pour two tablespoons of soap into the turmeric and mix until very smooth. Return this mixture back into the main batch and zap with your blender until you have reached trace. Pour this soap into your mould. (Alternatively use cupcake papers, as in the photograph opposite, and pour the soap at medium trace.)

7 Leave the soap to set for approximately 48 hours or until it has reached a 'hard cheese' consistency. Turn out of the mould and cut into bars. Cure the bars for four to six weeks before use.

INGREDIENTS

400 g (16 oz) coconut oil

150 g (6 oz) shea butter

200 g (8 oz) olive oil

200 g (8 oz) almond oil

50 g (2 oz) apricot kernel oil

330 g (13 oz) spring or distilled water

150 g (5¾ oz) sodium hydroxide

2 tbs turmeric

ESSENTIAL OILS

10 ml (2 tsp) geranium

2.5 ml (½ tsp) sweet orange

2.5 ml (½ tsp) mandarin

Superfatted at 3%

VARIATION

For really sensitive skin, try a blend of rose, lemon and Roman chamomile essential oils using 10 mls (2 tsp) total instead of 15 mls (3 tsp).

PACKAGING IDEA

To emphasize the gentleness of this soap, wrap it in handmade silk paper and tie it with silk ribbon.

SCRUB BARS

THE LIST OF INGREDIENTS YOU CAN PLAY with when making soap is virtually endless. In this section the soaps are designed around texture and purpose. You can choose mild exfoliation by adding botanicals such as dried herbs or rose petals, or for heavy scrubbing try adding coarse pumice, oatmeal or even sand.

The amount of exfoliating material you put in your soap is not critical – add as much or as little as you like – you can also replace one exfoliant with another. Why not experiment with the many grains you can find at the supermarket? Once you begin to think like a soap maker no food stuff, container or plant is safe!

Poppy seeds are not only decorative but are useful as an exfoliant, and you could also line your mould with a layer of tapioca or round beans as this will give you a massage bar. Try fruit seeds and ground kernels – strawberry and raspberry seeds work well and look pretty and ground olive stones are a vitamin-rich additive.

Rose and Oatmeal

This bar is packed with the goodness of dried rose petals and bran. Rose petals can be bought ready dried but it is a good idea to put them through a coffee grinder before use as whole petals can go slimy in your soap.

INGREDIENTS

500 g (20 oz) coconut oil

190 g (7½ oz) shea butter

300 g (12 oz) rapeseed (canola) oil

10 g (½ oz) wheatgerm oil

330 g (13 oz) spring or distilled water

15 g (1 tbs) powdered madder

151 g (6½ oz) sodium hydroxide

15 g (½ oz) ground oatmeal

8 g (½ oz) ground rose petals

10 ml (2 tsp) vitamin E oil

Dried rosebuds, for decoration

ESSENTIAL OILS

5 ml (1 tsp) geranium

2.5 ml (½ tsp) patchouli

2.5 ml (½ tsp) sweet orange

Superfatted at 3%

1 Weigh the coconut and shea butter, chop into small chunks and put in a plastic bucket. Weigh and add the rapeseed and wheatgerm oils.

2 Put on your rubber gloves and goggles. Weigh the water in a plastic bucket. Take 100 ml (3½ fl oz) water from the bucket, heat it slightly and pour it over the powdered madder. Weigh the sodium hydroxide in a jug.

3 Weigh out your oatmeal and your rose petals. Blend your essential oils and put them in with the oatmeal.

4 In a well ventilated area and wearing gloves, mask and goggles, pour the sodium hydroxide into the water, stir with a long handled, stainless steel spoon until dissolved then set aside. Remove mask.

5 Pour the caustic solution into the oils. Stir manually until the fats and oils have dissolved and then bring the soap to a light trace using a stick blender.

6 Add the vitamin E oil. Add the madder paste a spoonful at a time until you achieve the desired colour. Add the rose petals and oatmeal and mix in thoroughly with either a spoon or a blender and pour into prepared 1½ kg (3 lb) or individual moulds.

7 Leave the soap to set for approximately 48 hours or until it has reached a 'hard cheese' consistency. Turn out of the mould and cut into bars. Cure the bars for four to six weeks before use.

VARIATION

Directly after your bars are cut, push whole rosebuds into the surface of the soap. It is a good idea to dip these in melted candle wax first.

PACKAGING IDEA

Sprinkle loose rose petals over the surface of the soap and wrap it in clear cellophane.

Poppy Seed

I love using poppy seeds both as an exfoliant and for decoration. The heart mould I have used for this soap is a small silicone cake mould which I filled with a basic poppy seed soap and then put some seeds on the top.

1   Weigh the coconut and palm oils and shea butter, chop into small chunks and put in a plastic bucket. Weigh and add the olive oil.

2   Put on your rubber gloves and goggles. Weigh the water in a plastic bucket. Weigh the sodium hydroxide in a jug.

3   Weigh the poppy seeds. Blend the essential oils and put them in with the poppy seeds. (If you are making a layered soap keep half the essential oil back.)

4   In a well ventilated area and wearing gloves, mask and goggles, pour the sodium hydroxide into the water, stir with a long handled, stainless steel spoon until dissolved then set aside. Remove mask.

5   Pour the caustic solution into the oils. Stir manually until the fats and oils have dissolved and then bring the soap to a light trace using a stick blender. If you are making a layered soap, divide the batch into two jugs.

6   Add the colourant drop by drop into one of these jugs until the desired colour is achieved. Now add the remaining essential oil and zap with a blender until the soap reaches a heavy trace. Pour this soap into the mould.

7   Add the poppy seeds to the second jug, mix in thoroughly with either a spoon or a blender and pour into prepared moulds, or over the first layer of blue soap.

8   Leave the soap to set for approximately 48 hours or until it has reached a 'hard cheese' consistency. Turn out of the mould and cut into bars. Cure the bars for four to six weeks before use.

INGREDIENTS

400 g (16 oz) coconut oil

300 g (12 oz) palm oil

100 g (4 oz) shea butter

200 g (8 oz) olive oil

330 g (13 oz) spring or distilled water

151 g (6 oz) sodium hydroxide

8 g (⅓ oz) poppy seeds

2.5 ml (½ tsp) diluted ultramarine blue oxide (optional)

ESSENTIAL OILS

5 ml (1 tsp) ylang ylang

2.5 ml (½ tsp) howood

1 ml (¼ tsp) sweet orange

1 ml (¼ tsp) palmarosa

Superfatted at 3%

VARIATION

Replace the blue oxide with 3 tbs of cocoa powder mixed with a little water into a smooth paste. Use sweet orange, cinnamon and ginger essential oils.

PACKAGING IDEA

If you are cutting this soap into regular bars, place a slice of dried orange on top of the soap and secure with a raffia tie.

Gardeners' Soap

If you would prefer to use vegetable oils rather than lard to make a gardeners' soap, use any of the bar soap recipes in this book and substitute any exfoliant additives with pumice, using the essential oil blends suggested below.

INGREDIENTS

600 g (24 oz) lard

390 g (16 oz) rapeseed (canola) oil

10 g (½ oz) wheatgerm oil

330 g (13 oz) spring or distilled water

128 g (4¾ oz) sodium hydroxide

15 g (½ oz) coarse pumice

10 g (½ oz) vitamin E oil

ESSENTIAL OILS

5 ml (1 tsp) rosemary

2.5 ml (½ tsp) tea tree

2.5 ml (½ tsp) lavender

Superfatted at 3%

1 Weigh the lard, chop into small chunks and put in a plastic bucket. Weigh and add the rapeseed and wheatgerm oils.

2 Put on your rubber gloves and goggles. Weigh the water in a plastic bucket. Weigh the sodium hydroxide in a jug. Weigh out the pumice. Blend the essential oils and add to the pumice.

3 In a well ventilated area and wearing gloves, mask and goggles, pour the sodium hydroxide into the water, stir with a long handled, stainless steel spoon until dissolved then set aside. Remove mask.

4 Pour the caustic solution into the oils. Stir manually until the fats and oils have dissolved and then bring the soap to a light trace using a stick blender.

5 Add the vitamin E oil. Add the pumice and mix in thoroughly with either a spoon or a blender – you want a very thick mixture for a scrubby bar so add more pumice if the mix looks too thin. Pour into prepared 1½ kg (3 lb) moulds.

6 Leave the soap to set for approximately 48 hours or until it has reached a 'hard cheese' consistency. Turn out of the mould and cut into bars. Cure the bars for four to six weeks before use.

VARIATION

Try substitututing the pumice with cut luffa and the essential oils for a blend of lavender and lime.

PACKAGING IDEA

Cover a cardboard box with cut-up seed packets and put a soap and a Gardeners' Balm (see page 128) inside to make a great gardeners' gift.

PROVENÇAL

WHEN IT COMES TO SOAP INGREDIENTS, the French are truly blessed. A visit to Provence, with its acres of stunning lavender fields, will show you just how it got its reputation for wonderful fragrances. I live in the Dordogne, a south west region of France, and introducing handmade soaps to the French is a little like trying to sell refrigerators to Eskimos. Soap making is so much part of the culture that it is very hard to convince the French that there are alternative methods to the seven days of boiling and salting used to create their most famous soap, Savon de Marseille, originally made from pure olive oil.

The original Savon de Marseille soaps were un-perfumed and uncoloured. Here I give you my version of the original castile (olive oil) soap, which I proudly name *Savon de Ste Sabine* (see page 60). I have used the hot process method to make this soap, as well as *Laurus Nobilis* (see page 63), my version of *Savon d'Alep* (a traditional soap made with bay/laurel berry oil).

Lavender Provençal

Lavender outsells all varieties of soap by eight to one. Whole ranges of soaps and toiletries can be created using just this one plant and here I divide one batch into three to give you a variety of ways of presenting this perennial favourite.

INGREDIENTS

450 g (18 oz) coconut oil

500 g (20 oz) olive oil

50 g (2 oz) beeswax (flakes or granules)

330 g (13 oz) spring or distilled water

148 g (6 oz) sodium hydroxide

14 g (½ oz) dried lavender buds

10 ml (2 tsp) vitamin E oil

4 full lavender heads

10 ml (2 tsps) each blue and mauve oxide, diluted

ESSENTIAL OILS

15 ml (1 tbs) French lavender

Superfatted at 4%

1 Weigh the coconut, olive oil and beeswax and put in a stainless steel saucepan on a low heat to melt. Remove from heat as soon as melting point is reached.

2 Put on your rubber gloves and goggles. Weigh the water in a plastic bucket. Weigh the sodium hydroxide in a jug. Weigh the lavender buds and measure out the essential oils.

3 In a well ventilated area and wearing gloves, mask and goggles, pour the sodium hydroxide into the water, stir with a long handled, stainless steel spoon until dissolved then set aside. Remove mask.

4 Check the temperature of both the caustic solution and the oils, and when both reach approximately the same temperature pour the caustic solution into the oils. Stir manually for three minutes and then bring the soap to a light trace using a stick blender.

5 Add the vitamin E oil and the essential oil and stir to medium trace. Divide the batch equally between three jugs. Add the blue colourant drop by drop into one jug until the desired colour is achieved. Pour the soap into a mould.

6 Add the mauve colourant and the lavender buds to the second jug. Stir thoroughly and pour into a second mould. Leave the third batch plain – pour into the remaining mould then place the whole lavender heads on the top for decoration.

7 Leave the soap to set for approximately 48 hours or until the soap has reached a 'hard cheese' consistency. Turn out of the moulds and cut into bars. Cure the bars for four to six weeks before use.

VARIATIONS

To make a layered soap, add the colourants to each jug of soap in step 5. Bring the first jug to heavy trace with a blender and pour into your mould. Zap the second jug and pour this soap on the top. Pour the third layer on top without zapping.

PACKAGING IDEA

Place sprigs of lavender on top of the soap and wrap in cellophane. Alternatively package one of each soap in a white box with a clear acetate lid and tie with lavender-coloured ribbon and a tag. Soap shavings tied in muslin fabric can be sold as drawer fresheners.

Argile Clay

Originating in France, argile (or montmorillionite) clay is a kaolin powder that draws toxins out of the skin. Available in green, red, rose, yellow and white it also acts as a totally natural colourant and gives your soap a silky texture.

1 Weigh the coconut oil and shea butter, cut into small chunks and put in a plastic bucket. Weigh and add the rapeseed and olive oils.

2 Put on your rubber gloves and goggles. Weigh the water in a plastic bucket. Weigh the sodium hydroxide in a jug. Weigh the three clays. Measure out and blend together the essential oils, divide the blend in three and add to the clays in equal amounts. Add enough water to each clay to make a pourable paste.

3 In a well ventilated area and wearing gloves, mask and goggles, pour the sodium hydroxide into the water, stir with a long handled, stainless steel spoon until dissolved then set aside. Remove mask.

4 Pour the caustic solution into the oils. Stir manually until the fats and oils have dissolved and then bring the soap to a light trace using a stick blender.

5 Divide the batch equally between three jugs. Add one clay colour to each jug. Working quickly, zap the first jug with the blender taking care that the clay is distributed evenly. Pour into a prepared mould. Repeat for the other two jugs.

6 Leave the soaps to set for approximately 48 hours or until the soap has reached a 'hard cheese' consistency. Turn out of the moulds and cut into bars. Cure the bars for four to six weeks before use.

INGREDIENTS

400 g (16 oz) coconut oil

200 g (8 oz) shea butter

200 g (8 oz) rapeseed oil

200 g (8 oz) olive oil

330 g (13 oz) spring or distilled water

147 g (6 oz) sodium hydroxide

30 g (1½ oz) each of 3 different colours of Argile clay

ESSENTIAL OILS

5 ml (½ tsp) lavender

2 ml (½ tsp) cypress

1 ml (¼ tsp) sage

1 ml (¼ tsp) peppermint

Superfatted at 3%

VARIATION

For a deep, heady fragrance try ylang ylang, lavender and vetiver in equal quantities. For something a little spicier try ylang ylang and cinnamon.

PACKAGING IDEA

Make stripey coloured bands out of deckchair canvas, cut the short ends with pinking shears, wrap these around your soap and glue into place.

Savon de la Ste Sabine

Traditionally, the soap mixture for making Marseille soaps is boiled for many days, salted and then the soaps are dried for several months. To simplify this I have used the double boiler, hot process (HP) method. One great advantage with HP soaps is that they are mild enough to use straight away. The four week curing process is to allow the water to evaporate, thus creating a hard, long lasting bar. You need to use 35 per cent water in your formula as opposed to the 30–33 per cent used in the cold process.

INGREDIENTS

500 g (20 oz) coconut oil

500 g (20 oz) olive oil

350 g (14 oz) spring or distilled water

156 g (6¼ oz) sodium hydroxide

ESSENTIAL OILS

15 ml (1 tbs) any oils of your choosing

Superfatted at 2%

SPECIAL EQUIPMENT

2 stainless steel saucepans (one needs to fit inside the other to form a bain marie. The smaller pan should have a lid)

Mould (traditionally the finished soap should be a cube measuring approximately 9 cm/3½ in, so you need a mould that is at least 9 cm/3½ in high. This batch will make 2 soaps)

Sharp knife or cheesewire

1 Weigh the coconut and olive oils, put in the smaller stainless steel saucepan on a low heat to melt. Remove from heat as soon as melting point is reached.

2 Put on your rubber gloves and goggles. Weigh the water in a plastic bucket. Weigh the sodium hydroxide in a jug. Measure out the essential oils.

3 In a well ventilated area and wearing gloves, mask and goggles, pour the sodium hydroxide into the water, stir with a long handled, stainless steel spoon until dissolved then set aside. Remove mask.

4 Put a small bowl or wire rack inside the larger pot so that the smaller pot will not touch the bottom when placed inside (this is to prevent the soap from burning). Place the smaller pot in the larger one and fill the larger pot with water to the level of the oils. Remove the smaller pot and put the larger pot containing water on the heat to boil. You want to maintain a good simmer throughout the cooking process so you will need to keep topping up the outer pot with water.

5 Pour the caustic solution into the oils. Stir manually for three minutes and then bring the soap to a medium trace using a stick blender. Place the pot of soap inside the larger pot (on the heat). Cover the soap pot with a lid. You should now leave your soap to cook for one hour, topping up the water if necessary.

6 Meanwhile line your moulds with paper (HP soap is stickier than CP so it is difficult to get out of the mould unless you line it). The hot process takes between one and two hours depending on the formula and the size of the batch. It is ready for testing when the mixture has yellowed and become translucent like petroleum jelly.

7 Test the soap by taking a half teaspoonfull from the pot and rolling it into a ball. If it holds together and isn't too sticky your soap is ready. If not, it needs cooking for longer.

8 When the soap is cooked, remove it from the heat and add the essential oils, stirring in thoroughly. This is also the point where you should add colourant should you wish to. Pour the soap into the mould.

9 Leave the soap to set for approximately 48 hours or until the soap has reached a 'hard cheese' consistency. Turn out of the moulds and cut into blocks. You can make your soap look truly authentic by stamping it using woodblock carvings.

VARIATION

Include additives such as lavender buds in your soap at trace. Add natural colourants to your oils – alkanet for a purple-grey or annatto for sunny yellow.

PACKAGING IDEA

Wooden boxes designed for displaying wine bottles are great for packaging these soaps and also for using as moulds.

Laurus Nobilis

This is my version of *Savon d'Alep*, a therapeutic olive oil soap made in the Syrian city of Aleppo. Its base is pure pomace olive oil and up to 30 per cent laurel (bay) berry oil, which is said to ease arthritis and rheumatism. The oil has a wonderful natural scent so no additional fragrance is needed. I have used a regular hot process for my soap and in doing so have produced a mild, fragrant olive-coloured castile soap that is marbled through with white.

1 Weigh the olive and laurel oils and put in the smaller stainless steel saucepan.

2 Put on your rubber gloves and goggles. Weigh the water in a plastic bucket. Weigh the sodium hydroxide in a jug.

3 In a well ventilated area and wearing gloves, mask and goggles, pour the sodium hydroxide into the water, stir with a long handled, stainless steel spoon until dissolved then set aside. Remove mask.

4 Put a small bowl or wire rack inside the larger pot so that the smaller pot will not touch the bottom when placed inside. This is to prevent the soap burning. Place the smaller pot in the larger one and fill the larger pot with water to the level of the oils. Remove the smaller pot and put the larger pot containing water on the heat to boil. You want to maintain a good simmer throughout the cooking process so you will need to keep topping this pot up with water.

5 Pour the caustic solution into the oils. Stir manually for three minutes and then bring the soap to a medium trace using a stick blender. Place the pot of soap inside the larger pot (on the heat) and cover the inner pot with a lid.

6 You should now leave your soap to cook for 2½–3 hours, topping up the water in the large pot as it evaporates. When cooked, the soap will be green and almost translucent, although you may still have some soap that looks like mashed potatoes in there. Whilst you are waiting, line your moulds with paper.

7 Test the soap by dipping a teaspoon in the soap pot and putting your tongue against it. If your tongue tingles, you need to continue cooking. If the soap is ready it will taste of surprisingly fragrant pure soap. When the soap is cooked, remove it from the heat and simply tip it into your mould, banging the mould down to ensure an even spread.

8 Leave the soap to set for approximately 48 hours or until the soap has reached a 'hard cheese' consistency. Turn out of the mould and cut into blocks. Leave the soap to dry for at least two months. It may appear shrunken as the water evaporates but in the case of *Savon d'Alep*, that's a good thing!

INGREDIENTS

760 g (30 oz) olive oil

240 g (9½ oz) laurel (bay) berry oil

350 g (14 oz) spring or distilled water

131 g (5¼ oz) sodium hydroxide

350 g (14 oz) water

Superfatted at 2%

SPECIAL EQUIPMENT

2 stainless steel saucepans (one needs to fit inside the other to form a bain marie. The smaller pan should have a lid)

Mould (traditionally the finished soap should be a cube measuring approximately 9 cm/3½ in, so you need a mould that is at least 9 cm/3½ in high. This batch will make 2 soaps)

HOME SPA

WITH A BIT OF PREPARATION IT'S POSSIBLE to create a spa environment in your home – all you need is a deep, hot bath, lots of heavenly scented candles, some of your own homemade bath salts, scrubs and oils and the perfect soap for the occasion. Once you climb out of the bath you can smother yourself in your very own homemade body butter (see page 133), and what's more, you will know for certain that the ingredients in your products are the very best that money can buy and that you have not fallen into the trap of spending fortunes on a brand name.

The soaps in this section will detoxify, rejuvenate and stimulate your skin. They contain natural minerals such as Dead Sea mud and sea salt, along with pure soothing botanicals including aloe vera gel. All of these products, along with natural waxes, butters and plant extracts are widely available through soap making suppliers and each will add that very special 'spa experience' to your soap.

Seaweed and Aloe Vera

Seaweed is packed with vitamins and minerals and is a great additive for your soap. If you replace some of the water content with aloe vera juice or gel, the soap will soothe even the most sensitive of skins.

1 Weigh the coconut oil, cut into small chunks and put in a plastic bucket. Weigh and add the olive and hemp seed oils.

2 Put on your rubber gloves and goggles. Weigh the water in a plastic bucket. Weigh the sodium hydroxide in a jug. Weigh the kelp and dilute the oxide. Weigh the aloe vera. Measure out the essential oils and pour over the kelp.

3 In a well ventilated area and wearing gloves, mask and goggles, pour the sodium hydroxide into the water, stir with a long handled, stainless steel spoon until dissolved then set aside. Remove mask.

4 Pour the caustic solution into the oils. Stir manually until the fats and oils have dissolved and then bring the soap to a light trace using a stick blender. Add the kelp, the aloe vera and the colourant and stir thoroughly.

5 Pour into a 1½ kg (3 lb) prepared mould. Leave the soap to set for approximately 48 hours or until it has reached a 'hard cheese' consistency. Turn out of the mould and cut into bars. Cure the bars for four to six weeks before use.

INGREDIENTS

400 g (16 oz) coconut oil

400 g (16 oz) olive oil

200 g (8 oz) hemp seed oil

330 g (13 oz) spring or distilled water

150 g (6 oz) sodium hydroxide

50 g (2 oz) powdered kelp

15 ml (1 tbs) diluted green oxide

100 g (4 oz) aloe vera gel

ESSENTIAL OILS

10 ml (2 tsp) rosemary

5 ml (1 tsp) lavender

Superfatted at 3%

VARIATION

Replace the kelp with spirulina powder and use an essential oil blend of 10 ml (2 tsp) ylang ylang, 2½ ml (½ tsp) lemon and 2½ ml (½ tsp) gulab attar.

PACKAGING IDEA

Criss-cross hemp twine around the soap and knot. Thread the ends through two seashells and knot the twine to secure.

Sea Salt

Sea salt is a superb natural softener for your skin and, if used undiluted, is also an excellent exfoliant. For this recipe it is best to use medium to fine grains of salt as the large grains can be very scratchy.

1 Weigh the coconut and palm kernel oils and the cocoa butter, cut into small chunks and put in a plastic bucket. Weigh and add the olive oil.

2 Put on your rubber gloves and goggles. Weigh the water in a plastic bucket. Weigh the sodium hydroxide in a jug. Weigh the sea salt and dilute the oxide. Measure out the essential oils and pour them onto the sea salt.

3 In a well ventilated area and wearing gloves, mask and goggles, pour the sodium hydroxide into the water, stir with a long handled, stainless steel spoon until dissolved then set aside. Remove mask.

4 Pour the caustic solution into the oils. Stir manually until the fats and oils have dissolved and then bring the soap to a light trace using a stick blender. Add the colourant and stir thoroughly.

5 When the soap is at medium trace, stir in the salt/essential oil blend and pour into your prepared 1½ kg (3 lb) mould. Leave the soaps to set for approximately 48 hours or until the soap has reached a 'hard cheese' consistency. Turn out of the moulds and cut into bars. Cure the bars for four to six weeks before use.

INGREDIENTS

400 g (16 oz) coconut oil

300 g (12 oz) palm kernel oil

100 g (4 oz) cocoa butter

200 g (8 oz) olive oil

330 g (13 oz) spring or distilled water

157 g (5½ oz) sodium hydroxide

100 g (4 oz) fine or medium sea salt

15 ml (1 tbs) diluted blue oxide

ESSENTIAL OILS

10 ml (2 tsp) lemon tea tree

5 ml (1 tsp) sweet orange

Superfatted at 4%

VARIATIONS

Leave out the colouring and replace half of the salt with powdered kelp to make a green seaweed and sea salt combination.

PACKAGING IDEA

Wrap the soap in pale blue and white striped fabric or wallpaper and package together with a jar of Shea Butter Whip (see page 133).

Dead Sea Mud

Dead Sea mud stimulates blood circulation, hydrates the skin and is reputed to have anti-ageing qualities. Try it on the roots of your hair as it is known to strengthen them, and you could make a face mask with any left over mud.

INGREDIENTS

400 g (16 oz) coconut oil
50 g (2 oz) shea butter
100 g (4 oz) olive oil
250 g (10 oz) sunflower oil
264 g (10 oz) spring or distilled water
124 g (5 oz) sodium hydroxide
10 ml (2 tsp) vitamin E oil
100 g (4 oz) Dead Sea mud

ESSENTIAL OILS

10 ml (2 tsp) rosemary
5 ml (1 tsp) lavender

Superfatted at 3%

1 Weigh the coconut oil and shea butter, cut into small chunks and put in a plastic bucket. Weigh and add the olive and sunflower oils.

2 Put on your rubber gloves and goggles. Weigh the water in a plastic bucket. Weigh the sodium hydroxide in a jug. Weigh the mud. Measure out the essential oils and mix them with the mud.

3 In a well ventilated area and wearing gloves, mask and goggles, pour the sodium hydroxide into the water, stir with a long handled, stainless steel spoon until dissolved then set aside. Remove mask.

4 Pour the caustic solution into the oils. Stir manually until the fats and oils have dissolved and then bring the soap to a light trace using a stick blender. Add the vitamin E oil and the mud and stir to medium trace.

5 Pour the soap into a 1½ kg (3 lb) prepared mould. Leave the soap to set for approximately 48 hours or until it has reached a 'hard cheese' consistency. Turn out of the mould and cut into bars. Cure the bars for four to six weeks before use.

VARIATION

Add 5 g (¼ oz) of ground luffa as an exfoliant or pour the soap directly into a luffa and cut into slices when set.

PACKAGING IDEA

Package this soap in a drawstring bag together with the Shea Butter Whip (see page 133), a Bath and Body Oil (see page 137) and a slice of luffa.

OUT OF AFRICA

AFRICA OFFERS A WEALTH OF BOTANICAL wonders that can be included in soap recipes. Many of these plants, herbs and butters have been used for centuries by the local people to heal skin disorders and to protect the skin from the blistering sun.

The Marula tree has been a source of nutrition in Africa since 10,000 BC. In South Africa and Zimbabwe the oil, extracted from the fruit, is used as a skin cleanser and a baby oil. The oil produced from the seeds of the Baobab (or 'upside down') tree is rich in vitamins A and F — excellent for damaged skin — and Baobab powder can be used as a natural exfoliant.

Shea butter has incredible moisturizing benefits and soaps and creams made with cocoa butter have a wonderful richness. The Fairtrade movement has been a life changing force to the communities of mainly women who make their livelihoods from harvesting and processing these butters — particularly in Ghana and Tanzania — and our use of these exotic ingredients in our cosmetics means so much to Africa.

Baobab and Marula

The seeds of the Baobab tree (much loved by elephants) are full of edible goodness and the oil is superbly moisturizing and gentle in cosmetic products. Marula oil, extracted from the kernels, has an ideal composition of vitamins, minerals and fatty acids.

INGREDIENTS

500 g (20 oz) coconut oil
50 g (2 oz) shea butter
200 g (8 oz) sunflower oil
100 g (4 oz) baobab oil
150 g (6 oz) marula oil
330 g (13 oz) spring or distilled water
155 g (6 oz) sodium hydroxide

ESSENTIAL OILS

7½ ml (1½ tsp) rose geranium
5 ml (1 tsp) lavandin

Superfatted at 3%

1. Weigh the coconut oil and shea butter, cut into small chunks and put in a plastic bucket. Weigh and add the sunflower, baobab and marula oils.

2. Put on your rubber gloves and goggles. Weigh the water in a plastic bucket. Weigh the sodium hydroxide in a jug. Blend the essential oils.

3. In a well ventilated area and wearing gloves, mask and goggles, pour the sodium hydroxide into the water, stir with a long handled, stainless steel spoon until dissolved then set aside. Remove mask.

4. Pour the caustic solution into the oils. Stir manually until the fats and oils have dissolved and then bring the soap to a light trace using a stick blender.

5. Pour the soap into a 1½ kg (3 lb) mould. Leave the soap to set for approximately 48 hours or until it has reached a 'hard cheese' consistency. Turn out of the mould and cut into bars. Cure the bars for four to six weeks before use.

VARIATION

In Africa soap is used as much for its healing as its cleansing properties and 10 ml (2 tsp) of neem oil added to this recipe will help to heal cuts.

PACKAGING IDEA

Banana leaves and corn husks both make great packaging materials either nude from the tree or pulped and made into handmade paper.

Rooibos and Wild Honey

Rooibos is a herb that is unique to South Africa and sold worldwide as a tea. For the soap maker it offers anti-oxidant qualities. Honey is often used to help acne sufferers while beeswax gives your soap a hard waxy texture and makes it last longer.

1 Weigh the water and bring to the boil. Mix with the rooibos and the honey to make a tea. Leave to go cold. Sieve out the tea leaves and set them aside. Weigh the olive and palm kernel oils and the beeswax, and put them in a stainless steel saucepan on a low heat to melt. Remove from heat as soon as melting point is reached.

2 Put on your rubber gloves and goggles. Weigh the sodium hydroxide in a jug. Blend the essential oils.

3 In a well ventilated area and wearing gloves, mask and goggles, pour the sodium hydroxide into the rooibos and honey tea, stir with a long handled, stainless steel spoon until dissolved then set aside. Remove mask.

4 Check the temperature of both the caustic solution and the oils, and when both reach approximately the same temperature pour the caustic solution into the oils. Stir manually for three minutes and then bring the soap to a medium trace using a stick blender.

5 Add the essential oils and stir. If you want to add a handful of the brewed tea leaves this is the time to throw them into the pot. Stir until evenly distributed then pour the soap into a mould.

6 Leave the soap to set for approximately 48 hours or until it has reached a 'hard cheese' consistency. Turn out of the mould and cut into bars. Cure the bars for four to six weeks before use.

INGREDIENTS

330 g (13 oz) spring or distilled water
50 g (2 oz) Rooiboos tea
100 g (4 oz) honey
500 g (20 oz) olive oil
400 g (16 oz) palm kernel oil
100 g (4 oz) beeswax
135 g (5 oz) sodium hydroxide

ESSENTIAL OILS

10 ml (2 tsp) rosemary
2.5 ml (½ tsp) lavandin
2.5 ml (½ tsp) rose geranium

Superfatted at 3%

VARIATIONS

Honeybush tea can be substituted for the rooibos – try adding a blend of sweet orange, ylang ylang and a couple of drops of ginger and clove oil.

PACKAGING IDEA

Make use of brightly coloured African beads. Thread them on a leather thong or linen twine and tie around your soap. Present on a wooden soap dish.

Melon and Shea Butter

Watermelon seed oil comes from the Kalahari melon grown in dry rural regions of Africa, particularly in northern Namibia. Coupled with unrefined shea butter and coconut oil, it provides a highly moisturizing soap with a good, rich lather.

INGREDIENTS

400 g (16 oz) coconut oil

300 g (12 oz) shea butter

300 g (12 oz) watermelon seed oil

330 g (13 oz) spring or distilled water

147 g (5 oz) sodium hydroxide

ESSENTIAL OILS

2½ ml (½ tsp) tea tree

2½ ml (½ tsp) lavandin

2½ ml (½ tsp) rosemary

7½ ml (1½ tsp) sweet orange

Superfatted at 3%

1 Weigh the coconut oil and shea butter, cut into small chunks and put in a plastic bucket. Weigh and add the watermelon oil.

2 Put on your rubber gloves and goggles. Weigh the water in a plastic bucket. Weigh the sodium hydroxide in a jug. Blend the essential oils.

3 In a well ventilated area and wearing gloves, mask and goggles, pour the sodium hydroxide into the water, stir with a long handled, stainless steel spoon until dissolved then set aside. Remove mask.

4 Pour the caustic solution into the oils. Stir manually until the fats and oils have dissolved and then bring the soap to a light trace using a stick blender.

5 Pour the soap into 1½ kg (3 lb) prepared mould. Leave the soap to set for approximately 48 hours or until it has reached a 'hard cheese' consistency. Turn out of the mould and cut into bars. Cure the bars for four to six weeks before use.

VARIATION

For a heady, flowery scent use equal quantities of rose geranium, lavendin, and ylang ylang with a couple of drops of Roman camomile.

PACKAGING IDEA

Try wrapping this soap in banana leaves and use a strip of the leaf as a string to secure it. Corn husks also make interesting packaging.

African Black Soap

No section on Africa would be complete without reference to African black soap, known also as *alata* in Ghana and *ose dudu* in Nigeria. Black soap is produced in many rural communities throughout Africa from heavily-guarded recipes and has been prized for generations for its gentle moisturizing qualities.

The ingredients used in African black soap vary from region to region depending on what grows locally, but most comprise of either an olive-, palm kernel- or coconut-based oil hand-pressed within the villages. Where shea butter (karite) is available this is often included as a moisturizing additive. The uniqueness of African black soap is the fact that the lye is made by dripping rainwater through the ashes of roasted cocoa pods or plantain skins – not something most of us could try at home.

When lye is made in this fashion it is very difficult to measure the density and the resulting solution is closer to potassium hydroxide (used to made liquid soap) than sodium hydroxide (used for bar soaps) and as a result, true African black soap is often soft and malleable. It is also sometimes diluted and sold as a liquid soap for use as a shampoo. That said, you can find on the market a number of hard bar soaps originating in Africa that describe themselves as 'African black soap'. These are still a long way from the traditional village soaps that are created with much pride and joy in 'soap kettles', where the lye and the fats/oils and water are boiled together over an open fire until the soap raises to the surface and is skimmed off and formed into balls or rough blocks.

FESTIVE SOAPS

SOAPS AND TOILETRIES MAKE GREAT gifts and for those who plan to run a soap making business you will find that you sell more soaps during festive seasons than at any other time of the year. The only problem is the stacks of Christmas pudding or pumpkin shaped soaps you will find filling up your shelves the day after the holiday.

However there is a simple solution. Make your soaps using traditional Christmas fragrances, such as cinnamon, orange and clove; use as much pumpkin oil as you like in your Thanksgiving soap; but, with the exception of heart shapes (which boom around St. Valentines day and do well right through the year), stick to oblongs and squares and use only your packaging to express the festivities.

That way you can repackage spicy smelling soaps after the event to suggest a season-proof oriental theme, and you can promote your pumpkin soap by highlighting the anti-oxidant elements of pumpkin seed oil (you could even repackage this soap for pregnant mums as pumpkin seed oil is great for stretch marks). Problem solved.

Christmas Spice

The rich scents of cinnamon, orange and clove are synonymous with Christmas and lovely to have in your bathroom to welcome holiday guests. Be aware that soaps containing clove oil trace very quickly so have your moulds ready before you mix your soap.

INGREDIENTS

400 g (16 oz) coconut oil

300 g (12 oz) olive oil

100 g (4 oz) watermelon oil

200 g (8 oz) shea butter

330 g (13 oz) spring or distilled water

147 g (5 oz) sodium hydroxide

100 g (4 oz) cocoa powder

Dried orange slice or cinnamon stick, to decorate (optional)

ESSENTIAL OILS

10 ml (2 tsp) sweet orange

2.5 ml (½ tsp) cinnamon

2.5 ml (½ tsp) clove

Superfatted at 4%

1 Weigh the coconut oil and chop into small chunks. Weigh the olive and watermelon oils and the shea butter and put in a plastic bucket.

2 Put on your rubber gloves and goggles. Weigh the water in a plastic bucket. Weigh the sodium hydroxide in a jug.

3 Measure out the essential oils and blend together. Measure out the cocoa powder. Make a paste by adding around 1 tbs of water. Add the essential oil blend to the cocoa paste.

4 In a well ventilated area and wearing gloves, mask and goggles, pour the sodium hydroxide into the water, stir with a long handled, stainless steel spoon until dissolved then set aside. Remove mask.

5 Pour the caustic solution into the oils. Stir manually until the fats and oils have dissolved and then bring the soap to a light trace using a stick blender. Add the cocoa powder and stir thoroughly.

6 Pour the soap into a 1½ kg (3 lb) mould. Leave the soap to set for approximately 48 hours or until it has reached a 'hard cheese' consistency. Turn out of the mould and cut into bars.

7 Press the dried orange or the cinnamon stick into the surface of your soap, if using. If it won't stick, wet the surface of the soap slightly. Cure the bars for four to six weeks before use.

VARIATION

Replace the cinnamon and clove essential oils with the same quantities of frankincense and myrrh essential oils.

PACKAGING IDEA

Instead of cutting the soap into bars, roll into balls (wearing rubber gloves), tie a ribbon around and stick cloves into the surface to form a pomander.

Bollywood

During a particularly creative week I dressed my soaps as Indian princesses in fine silk fabric and jewelled bindis. Harrods of London made an order for a range of similarly attired soaps, lotions and balms and this is the soap I created for them.

1 Weigh the coconut and palm oils and the shea butter, chop into small chunks and put in a plastic bucket. Weigh and add the olive oil.

2 Put on your rubber gloves and goggles. Weigh the water in a plastic bucket. Weigh the sodium hydroxide in a jug. Measure out the essential oils and blend them together. Dilute the colourant.

3 In a well ventilated area and wearing gloves, mask and goggles, pour the sodium hydroxide into the water, stir with a long handled, stainless steel spoon until dissolved then set aside. Remove mask.

4 Pour the caustic solution into the oils. Stir manually until the fats and oils have dissolved and then bring the soap to a light trace using a stick blender. Add the colourant and the essential oil blend and stir thoroughly

5 Pour the soap into a 1½ kg (3 lb) mould. Leave the soap to set for approximately 48 hours or until it has reached a 'hard cheese' consistency. Turn out of the mould and cut into bars. Stick the bindis into place. Cure the bars for four to six weeks before use.

INGREDIENTS

400 g (16 oz) coconut oil

100 g (4 oz) palm oil

200 g (8 oz) shea butter

300 g (12 oz) olive oil

330 g (13 oz) spring or distilled water

148 g (6 oz) sodium hydroxide

ESSENTIAL OILS

5 ml (1 tsp) rose geranium

2.5 ml (½ tsp) frankincense

2 ml (½ tsp) ylang ylang

1.5 ml (¼ tsp) mandarin

1 ml (¼ tsp) cinnamon

1 ml (¼ tsp) bergamot

1 ml (¼ tsp) lemon

1 ml (¼ tsp) gulab attar

COLOURANT

D&C colourant or oxide of your choice – dilute 1 ml (¼ tsp) D&C colourant in 20 ml (4 tsp) water or 5 ml (1 tbs) oxide in 30 mls (6 tsp) water and add drop by drop at trace until you achieve the desired colour

Superfatted at 4%

VARIATION

Just after cutting the soap, sprinkle a metallic mica powder onto the surface and substitute the fabric for gold or silver paper.

PACKAGING IDEA

Package this soap together with a Bath and Body Oil (see page 137) and a Bath Melt (see page 134) in a foil box with an acetate lid.

I Do

Weddings are big business. Offering to make favours is a great way of showing off your soap making skills and building your client list. In this recipe I have used pure silk fabric as it really does make the soap feel silky.

INGREDIENTS

400 g (16 oz) coconut oil
300 g (12 oz) olive oil
100 g (4 oz) hemp seed oil
100 g (4 oz) sweet almond oil
100 g (4 oz) cocoa butter, grated
330 g (13 oz) spring or distilled water
149 g (6 oz) sodium hydroxide
Gold mica (optional)

ESSENTIAL OILS

10 ml (2 tsp) sweet orange
2.5 ml (½ tsp) geranium
2.5 ml (½ tsp) palmarosa

COLOURANT

D&C colourant or oxide of your choice – dilute 1 ml (¼ tsp) D&C colourant in 20 ml (4 tsp) water or 5 ml (1 tbs) oxide in 30 mls (6 tsp) water and add drop by drop at trace until you achieve a pastel tint

SPECIAL EQUIPMENT

20 cm (8 in) square of undyed silk
Fancy silicone ice cube trays

Superfatted at 4%

1 Weigh the coconut oil, chop it into small chunks and put it in a plastic bucket. Weigh and add the olive, hemp seed and sweet almond oils and the cocoa butter.

2 Weigh the water in a plastic bucket. Weigh the sodium hydroxide in a jug. Measure out the essential oils and blend together. Dilute the colourant

3 In a well ventilated area and wearing gloves, mask and goggles, pour the sodium hydroxide into the water, stir with a long handled, stainless steel spoon until dissolved. Add the piece of silk to the lye solution and stir until dissolved then set aside. Remove mask.

4 Pour the caustic solution into the oils. Stir manually until the fats and oils have dissolved and then bring the soap to a light trace using a stick blender. Add the essential oil blend and stir thoroughly. Now add the colourant drop by drop until you achieve the desired colour.

5 Pour the soap into silicone ice cube trays. Leave the soaps to set for approximately 48 hours or until they have reached a 'hard cheese' consistency. Turn out of the mould. Sprinkle powdered gold mica onto the surface of the soaps. Cure the soaps for four to six weeks before use.

VARIATION

Split the batch into two jugs at trace and add blue colourant to one jug and pink to the second. Pour into two separate moulds.

PACKAGING IDEA

Wrap the soaps in silk paper and tie with silk ribbon or put three or four in a small voile bag.

SPECIAL EFFECTS

SPECIAL EFFECTS CAN BE ACHIEVED through changes and combinations of colour, shape, presentation and purpose and also by using any one of the thousands of decorative items available in craft shops as well as on beaches, in forests and food stores.

COLOUR

There are both natural and artificial ways to colour your soap (see pages 18–19). The colour of your base oils will affect the final colour but the best way to experiment is to make a plain batch of soap and to divide it at light trace into several jugs, colouring each one with a different oxide, pigment, spice or infused oil. The following recipe will give you a neutral-coloured soap base to play with:

400 g (16 oz) coconut oil

300 g (12 oz) palm oil

300 g (12 oz) sunflower oil

330 g (13 oz) water

152 g (6 oz) sodium hydroxide

SWIRLS

To achieve a good swirl in your soap, divide the batch into three parts base colour and one part contrasting colour. Pour a layer of base into your mould and then pour lines of your contrasting colour over the top. Swirl the soap together by running a skewer or a fork through the coloured lines. Add another layer of the base and more lines of colour and swirl again. Repeat until all the soap is used up. Good swirls come from plenty of practice and different effects can be achieved by 'pulling' the colour in different directions.

LAYERS

Using a loaf or box mould you can make endless layers of different colours by pouring soaps directly on top of each other. It is important to ensure that each layer is firm enough to support the layer on top so your bottom layer needs to have reached a very heavy trace before the next layer is added. One way to achieve this is to divide and colour your soaps at a very light trace. Using a stick blender, zap the jug containing the soap you want to use for your base layer until it is very thick and then scrape it into your mould. By this time your second jug of soap will have begun to thicken and you can pour this directly on top. If you are planning on building three layers, zap the contents of the second jug as well so that the soap will be thick enough to support your third layer.

LANDSCAPE SOAP

Wonderful landscape and seascape effects, such as in the soap on the left, can be achieved by pouring random amounts of differently coloured or textured soaps into a loaf mould at heavy trace. To create a seascape, start with a yellow or neutral coloured soap and add some oatmeal for texture. Pour this into the mould. Now pour some blues or greens (or both) in lines and blobs over the oatmeal layer until the soap is about 5 cm (2 in) deep in total. Your next layer is for the sky and could be made with pale blue or grey (alkanet) soap with random blobs of white soap (for clouds), and perhaps some pink lines to give a sunrise effect. You also want a thick line of yellow or red soap poured along one long edge of the mould to form the sun. When planning your design you need to think about how a stick of rock candy works. Patterns are formed in long strips that run right through the rock – when placing your colours remember that the soap will be sliced and so you need the colour to run right through the mould.

The best landscape soaps are made by accident. On soap making day, keep an empty loaf mould to hand and fill it with the scrapings from each batch of soap you make, positioning them in random blobs or thin layers as the fancy takes you. You can keep adding to the mould as you make different coloured soaps and you will be amazed at the beautiful effects you can achieve. You can keep a mould going in this way for up to a week, any longer and the different soap layers may not hold together well as the soap in the mould will be too hard. Remember that if you are planning to sell your landscape soaps you need to work with just one base formula and ensure that all the colourants/additives you use are on your assessment (see pages 138–141) and also listed on your labels.

SHAPE

The shape of your soap is determined by the shape of your mould or your cutting device. If you want fancy shapes the best results will be achieved using flexible silicone or latex moulds and these are made not only for soap making but for garden ornaments, architectural features, candles, model making and numerous other arts and crafts.

The cupid plaque in the illustration was made using a mould intended for a concrete slab. I thought it would be fun to create a soap plaque that you could hang in the shower the idea being

that instead of bringing the soap to your body you fill your sponge with soap by rubbing it on the soap plaque. Once the soap is hard you need only drill a couple of holes in it and you can hang it in the shower on a cord. Another way of displaying it would be to make a box frame it can sit in and then you can refill this with a fresh soap plaque when your soap 'fixture' begins to wear too thin.

Liquid Soaps

THE BASICS

IF YOU ARE PLANNING TO START YOUR
own soap making business it is worth mastering
the art of liquid soap making as liquid soaps
outsell bar soaps eight to one. There are several
ways to make liquid soap, but the main method
used in this book is the paste method. Using a
double boiler oils are saponified with potassium
hydroxide and cooked together for several hours
until they form a glutinous soap gel. The gel is
then diluted with water and essential oils and
colourants are added. Compared to bar soap
making this process is quite long winded but
the advantages are firstly that the soap paste can
be stored in a cool place for up to a year before
dilution, and secondly the soap is ready to use
as soon as it is cooked.

Any product containing water can attract
bacteria and for this reason you will find that the
pH value of most natural liquid soaps is relatively
high at around 10.3, and considerably higher
if the soaps do not contain a preservative. A
high pH helps reduce the possibility of bacteria
forming and whilst some essential oils will help
to preserve your product, there is, at the time
of writing, no truly effective natural preservative
available. Due to the high pH a natural liquid
soap is probably more suitable as a hand soap
than a face soap.

The second method involves cooking oils,
potassium hydroxide and alcohol together.
Whilst the alcohol speeds up the saponification
process this is a tricky method to use at home as
alcohol and kitchen cookers (especially gas ones)
are a potential recipe for disaster.

The third and speediest method of making
liquid soap is to dissolve cold or hot processed
soaps in boiling water. Depending how much
water you use you can achieve a relatively thick
liquid soap but it does have a tendency to form a
skin, and you cannot make a clear soap using this
simple method.

FATS AND OILS (ACIDS)

The choice of oils and fats is infinite but the
quality of the soap you produce will depend on
this choice. When formulating a liquid soap
your main consideration is to create a mild,
clear soap with rich bubbles. For both clarity and
lather coconut oil is a good choice. It has a large
proportion of lauric acid which is highly soluble
and as such will contribute greatly to the clarity of
the soap and to the quality of the lather. However
a soap containing 100 per cent coconut oil can
be very drying on the skin so this needs to be
balanced with other oils.

On pages 10–14 you will find a full description
of the properties of the oils most commonly
used in soap and cosmetics and from this list
you can select other oils for your formula,
depending on what you want to achieve. Both
olive and sunflower oils are great for bulking-
out the formula and are both mild and
emollient. Castor oil will give you a good foam
and is a great choice for both a shaving soap and
a shampoo, but for gentleness you could include
(in small quantities) moisturizing oils such as
avocado, apricot kernel and shea butter.

POTASSIUM HYDROXIDE (ALKALI)

It is very important that the correct amount of
alkali is used to saponify the oils you have selected.
If you look at the saponifcation chart on page
25 you will see two sets of numbers (SAP values)
next to each oil. When making liquid soap we

use potassium hydroxide (KOH) as opposed to sodium hydroxide (NaOH), so the KOH values are the ones to use. See page 24 for instructions on multiplying the weight of oil or fat by KOH.

MAKING LIQUID SOAP

Liquid soap is made using a hot process method. As you are using a powerful alkali to saponify your oils, it is important that you treat the alkali with respect and follow all the safety measures described on page 23. Remember to always wear rubber gloves and eye protection when working with lye or fresh soap and wear a face mask when pouring the lye into the water. Take care to accurately weigh out all fats and oils and water and lye. For liquid soap calculate 35 per cent of the weight of the oils and use that amount of water in the lye solution. You also have the option of replacing some of that water content with aloe vera gel.

The lye water is then added to the oils and mixed with a stick blender until the mixture has emulsified (traced). This process takes considerably longer using potassium hydroxide than sodium hydroxide so don't panic if the mixture doesn't seem to be tracing, just keep going. Once the mixture is creamy, put the soap pot into a larger pot containing water (bain marie), and then place on the heat to cook for around three hours at a rolling boil.

POTASSIUM CARBONATE

During the cooking process, the soap goes through a number of stages. For the first 30 minutes the mixture will appear to separate and even curdle, but keep stirring every ten minutes until it comes together. Once this happens the soap will begin to resemble apple sauce, quickly followed by mashed potato, and then it turns to thick toffee which can be almost impossible to stir. After a period of around three hours (depending on your batch size) the sticky toffee will turn translucent and resemble deep yellow petroleum jelly. At this point your soap is ready.

The sticky toffee stage is manageable with small batches of soap but if you are making a large batch you could find yourself neck deep in a gluey mess trying to stir the soap at the bottom of the pot. To avoid this situation I use potassium carbonate in all my liquid soap formulas. While it is also an alkali, it has the magic property of keeping your soap mixable right through the process. This is a real life saver for large batches but the downside is that if you mix alkalis together it takes longer to reach trace and separation is more likely to occur. Once again, just keep stirring and the mixture will blend together.

To calculate how much potassium carbonate to use simply add together the weight of the oils and add carbonate at 2 per cent of that weight.

SUPERFATTING

It is not advisable to superfat a liquid soap because free oils plus water can equal bacteria. However, potassium carbonate is an alkali and to ensure your soap remains mild it is necessary to make an adjustment for it when working out how much potassium hydroxide you need in your formula. If you are working out the amount of potassium hydroxide you need from the chart on page 25 simply deduct 2 per cent from the total. Alternatively, if you are using an online SAP calculator (see Internet Resources on page 143) set the superfatting option to 2 per cent.

TESTING

Once your soap has turned translucent, you should test it for clarity and mildness. To do this, take a small spoonful of soap from the pot and weigh it, then put it in a glass or plastic tumbler. You should now dilute this in twice its weight of boiling water (i.e. for 14 g / ½ oz soap paste add 28 g / 1 oz boiling water). If the soap is ready the dissolved solution should be clear. You can also test it for mildness using pH papers. If the soap is ready the paper will indicate a pH of below 10.5.

DILUTING

The paste you have made is a highly concentrated pure soap and this can be transformed into a liquid consistency by adding boiled spring or distilled water. My personal preference is 2 parts water to one part soap paste as this produces a stable, cleansing soap that works well in a pump applicator. It is reasonable to assume that if you use less water your soap will be thicker, but in fact using less water simply gives you a stronger concentration of soap. You can dilute as much or as little of the soap paste as you like, storing any excess in a plastic lidded tub. Simply weigh the amount of paste you want to dilute and add twice the amount of boiling spring water. Do not stir (this will introduce bubbles), just cut the paste with a knife to speed up the process. Soap dilution can take quite a long time especially for large batches so it is best to add the boiling water, cover the pot and leave it overnight. If the soap has not fully dissolved by the morning heat it gently and cut any remaining paste until the process is complete.

NEUTRALISING

Once your soap has dissolved, check the pH again. If it is over 10.5 you can neutralize it with a citric acid formula. Dissolve 1 part citric acid in 4 parts water and, using a pipette, add this solution to your soap until the pH drops to under 10.

FRAGRANCING

Liquid soap can be fragranced with up to 2 per cent essential or fragrance oils. Warm the diluted soap to just above room temperature before adding fragrance. At this stage you can also add a few drops of liquid cosmetic or food colourant but be aware that a little goes a long way. Some essential oils will cloud your soap initially but this will settle.

PRESERVING

Any product containing water has the potential to attract bacteria, but bacteria is often introduced into products such as creams and lotions by dipping your fingers in the pot. Liquid soaps are usually packaged in sealed pump applicators which reduce the risk of bacteria entering the product, and there are a number of natural liquid soaps on the market that rely entirely on a pH of around 10 and the use of anti-bacterial essential oils such as tea tree or rosemary to fight the possibility of bacteria.

The choice is yours but if you intend to sell your soap you should consider using one of the non-paraben based preservatives on the market. There are a number of cosmetic preservatives on offer but before making a selection you need to remember that you are working with a high pH and many preservatives are not designed for this. My preservative of choice is Optiphen, which is a paraben- and formaldehyde-free blend of phenoxyethanol and Capryl glycol. ND is the Optiphen grade needed for liquid soap and I have found it works well at 1 per cent. It is widely available through distributors in the UK and in the USA (see Stockists on page 143).

THICKENING

Whilst the quality of your natural liquid soap will be extremely high, it may tend to be thinner than mass produced liquid detergents. Typical thickening agents such as agar, guar gum and carrageenan do not work well in products with a high pH and tend to turn liquid soap gloopy. Outside Europe, borax is widely used for both its thickening and chelating properties but it is restricted under EU legislation as it known to irritate the skin. Some soap makers use salt as a natural thickener and you can also replace up to 4 per cent of your potassium hydroxide with sodium hydroxide during the paste formation to assist with thickening, although I have not had much success with this.

The best thickener I have is a cellulose gum made from plant fibres. If diluting 50 g (2 oz) of soap paste, sprinkle up to third of a teaspoon cellulose gum into 150 g (5 oz) boiling water and whisk thoroughly. Add this water to your soap paste to dilute it. You can adjust the quantity of gum according to how thick you want your soap. If you intend to put your soap into a foam pump, do not attempt to thicken it as it will clog up the mechanism.

BOTTLING
Once your diluted soap is cool, sterilize your bottles with boiling water, pour the soap into the bottle and seal.

EQUIPMENT
Double boiler (Bain Marie)
Two stainless steel pots, one to fit inside the other so water can be boiled in the outer pot. The smaller pot needs a tight fitting lid.
Kitchen scales weighing in very small increments. You need specialist scales if you are making soap to sell.
Long handled, stainless steel spoon
Knife to cut fats
Stick blender
Plastic bucket
Plastic jugs x 2
Rubber spatula
Plastic lidded container to store the paste in
Pump bottles for the finished soap
Rubber gloves
Eye goggles
Dust mask
Vinegar

INGREDIENTS
Oils and fats of your choice
Potassium hydroxide
Potassium carbonate (optional)
Spring or distilled water
Citric acid
Preservative (optional)

COOKING LIQUID SOAP
1. Melt the oils and add the lye mixture. Stir until the mixture forms an emulsion then put in a bain marie.
2. The soap will go through an 'apple sauce' stage.
3. Eventually the soap will become translucent and resemble yellow petroleum jelly. Test the for clarity and mildness and then dilute.

Basic Liquid Soap Paste

This recipe will produce a gentle, clear, all-purpose soap. You can add whatever essential oils you like, perhaps tea tree for a kitchen soap or a geranium and lavender combination for something a little more feminine.

1 Weigh the coconut, sunflower and olive oils and put them in a stainless steel saucepan. Weigh the water and pour into a plastic bucket. Half fill the larger saucepan with tap water and put it on the heat.

2 Put on your gloves, goggles and mask. Weigh the potassium hydroxide and potassium carbonate separately and then combine. Add the potassium hydroxide and potassium carbonate mixture to the water and stir for two minutes.

3 Melt the oils on a low heat and stir. Remove the soap pot from the heat. Still wearing your protective kit, pour the alkali mixture into the pot and stir again. Bring the soap to trace using a stick blender. (The oils and liquids may separate – keep mixing until they come together again.)

4 Place the soap pot into the larger pot and bring the water to a rolling boil. Cover the pot. Top up water in outer pot as it evaporates. Stir every 15 minutes for approximately three hours or until the mixture in the pot resembles deep yellow petroleum jelly.

5 Remove from the heat and test (see page 95). If the soap is ready, store in a plastic lidded container or dilute as per the instructions below. If not continue to cook until it tests clear.

DILUTION

To fill a 250 ml (8 fl oz) container, weigh 83 g (3 oz) of soap paste and dilute with 166 ml (6 oz) boiling spring water. Once dissolved, heat until tepid and add up to 2.5 ml (½ tsp) essential oil of your choice. Also add preservative at this stage, should you require it, following the manufacturer's recommended ratio. Allow to cool and then pour into a sterilized bottle.

INGREDIENTS FOR UNDILUTED SOAP PASTE

200 g (8 oz) coconut oil

200 g (8 oz) sunflower oil

100 g (4 oz) olive oil

180 g (7 oz) spring water

108 g (4 oz) potassium hydroxide

10 g (½ oz) potassium carbonate

97

Shaving Mousse

Light, foaming mousses are created by putting your liquid soap into a foam pump applicator. This formula is smooth, moisturizing and rich in bubbles. Fragrance with cedarwood for men and geranium and mandarin for a floral feminine scent.

INGREDIENTS FOR UNDILUTED SOAP PASTE

300 g (12 oz) coconut oil

100 g (4 oz) castor oil

100 g (4 oz) olive oil

180 g (7 oz) spring water

112 g (4½ oz) potassium hydroxide

10 g (⅓ oz) potassium carbonate

1 Weigh the coconut, castor and olive oils and put them in a stainless steel saucepan. Weigh the water and pour into a plastic bucket. Half fill the larger saucepan with tap water and put it on the heat.

2 Put on your gloves, goggles and mask. Weigh the potassium hydroxide and potassium carbonate separately and then combine. Add the potassium hydroxide and potassium carbonate mixture to the water in the bucket and stir for two minutes.

3 Melt the oils on a low heat and stir. Remove the soap pot from the heat. Still wearing your protective kit, pour the alkali mixture into the pot and stir again. Bring the soap to trace using a stick blender. (The oils and liquids may separate – keep mixing until they come together again.)

4 Place the soap pot into the larger pot and bring the water to a rolling boil. Cover the pot. Top up the water in the outer pot as it evaporates. Stir every 15 minutes for approximately three hours or until the mixture in the pot has resembles deep yellow petroleum jelly.

5 Remove from the heat and test (see page 95). If the soap is ready, store in a plastic lidded container or dilute as per instructions on page 97. If not, continue to cook until it tests clear. Sterilize the foamer bottle.

Family Shampoo

In hard water areas, use diluted lemon juice or cider vinegar as a final rinse to restore balance. Those with dry hair can use a natural conditioner after cleansing such as pure shea butter – rub into the roots, leave for ten minutes and then rinse off.

1 Weigh the coconut, olive, castor, shea and jojoba oils and put them in a stainless steel saucepan. Weigh the water and pour into a plastic bucket. Half fill your larger saucepan with tap water and put it on the heat.

2 Put on your gloves, goggles and mask. Weigh the potassium hydroxide and potassium carbonate separately and then combine. Add the potassium hydroxide and potassium carbonate mixture to the water and stir for two minutes.

3 Melt the oils on a low heat and stir. Remove the soap pot from the heat. Still wearing your protective kit, pour the alkali mixture into the pot and stir again. Bring the soap to trace using a stick blender. (The oils and liquids may separate – keep mixing until they come together again.)

4 Place the soap pot into the larger pot and bring water the to a rolling boil. Cover the pot. Top up the water in the outer pot as it evaporates. Stir every 15 minutes for approximately three hours or until the mixture in the pot resembles deep yellow petroleum jelly.

5 Remove from the heat and test (see page 95). If the soap is ready, store in a plastic lidded container or dilute as per the instructions below. If not, continue to cook until it tests clear.

DILUTING, FRAGRANCING AND THICKENING

For a 250 ml (8 fl oz) bottle of shampoo, sprinkle 1 tsp of cellulose acetate into 166g (6 oz) of boiling water and whisk. Add 83 g (3 oz) of soap paste and leave to dissolve, stirring from time to time. Heat the mixture to tepid, add a drop of colouring (if required) then add your chosen essential oil blends.

INGREDIENTS FOR UNDILUTED SOAP PASTE

200 g (8 oz) coconut oil

210 g (8½ oz) olive oil

50 g (2 oz) castor oil

20 g (1 oz) shea oil

20 g (1 oz) jojoba oil

180 g (7 oz) water

104 g (4¼ oz) potassium hydroxide

10 g (⅓ oz) Potassium carbonate

1 drop food colourant per 250 g (10 oz) diluted soap

VARIATIONS

NORMAL HAIR	GREASY HAIR	DRY HAIR	FINE HAIR	ANTI-DANDRUFF
12 drops lemon	24 drops basil	36 drops lavender	48 drops chamomile	48 drops peppermint
24 drops geranium	24 drops lemon	24 drops rosemary	12 drops lavender	12 drops sage
24 drops parsley	12 drops thyme			

Shampoodle

I use this recipe as a dog wash for my two poodles. The essential oil blend will help to deter fleas. You can moisturize a dog coat by rubbing in some shea butter before the final rinse.

INGREDIENTS FOR UNDILUTED SOAP PASTE

200 g (8 oz) coconut oil

200 g (8 oz) canola (rapeseed) oil

100 g (4 oz) olive oil

180 g (7 oz) spring water

103 g (4 oz) potassium hydroxide

10 g (⅓ oz) potassium carbonate

1 Weigh the coconut, canola and olive oils and put them in a stainless steel saucepan. Weigh the water and pour into a plastic bucket. Half fill the larger saucepan with tap water and put it on the heat.

2 Put on your gloves, goggles and mask. Weigh the potassium hydroxide and potassium carbonate separately and then combine. Add the potassium hydroxide and potassium carbonate mixture to the water and stir for two minutes.

3 Melt the oils on a low heat and stir. Remove the soap pot from the heat. Still wearing your protective kit, pour the alkali mixture into the pot and stir again. Bring the soap to trace using a stick blender. (The oils and liquids may separate – keep mixing until they come together again.)

4 Place the soap pot into the larger pot and bring the water to a rolling boil. Cover the pot. Top up the water in the outer pot as it evaporates. Stir every 15 minutes for approximately three hours or until the mixture in the pot resembles deep yellow petroleum jelly.

5 Remove from the heat and test (see page 95). If the soap is ready, store in a plastic lidded container or dilute as per the instructions on page 97. If not, continue to cook until it tests clear.

VARIATIONS

BLEND ONE

36 drops cedarwood

24 drops lavender

BLEND TWO

24 drops citronella

24 drops thyme

12 drops lavender

Rebatched Liquid Soap

If you don't want to make your liquid soap from scratch you have two options: you can rebatch all your leftover bits of bar soap or you can dilute the soap paste you produce when you are making hot processed soap. Both methods are given below.

FROM SOAP SCRAPS

1 Grate the soap scraps and put in a jug. Boil 200 g (7 oz) of the water and pour it over the soap. Whisk until dissolved.

2 Add the remaining water and glycerine and mix with a stick blender until smooth. (Add more spring water at room temperature to make the soap thinner, if desired.) Allow to cool and then pour into a sterilized bottle.

FROM HOT PROCESS SOAP PASTE

1 When making bar soap using the hot process method (such as Laurus Nobilis on page 63), pour a couple of tablespoons of soap paste into a jug before pouring the rest into a mould.

2 Add three parts boiling water to one part paste and leave to dissolve. This makes a wonderful thick, castile liquid soap.

INGREDIENTS

100g (4 oz) cold process soap scraps

300g (12 oz) distilled or spring water

1 tsp glycerine

Creams, Balms, Whips and Melts

THE BASICS

IF WE BELIEVE WHAT WE ARE TOLD BY the world of advertising, there is a cream available for absolutely everything. There are different creams, lotions and balms for different parts of our body, for day and night, and many of these products come with a terrifying price tag. However, there are in fact only two types of cream – heavy creams, which are absorbed slowly to form a protective barrier (night creams, creams with a healing element, foot creams and cleansers); and light creams which absorb quickly (day moisturizers and lotions). Lotions are simply diluted creams and balms are blends of fats, oils and waxes that do not contain water.

All creams are a combination of botanical oils, essential oils and water and are designed to penetrate and nourish the surface of the skin. Water and oils will not blend together so a vegetable-based emulsifier is used to enable blending. Vegetable-based cetyl alcohol is also used to stabilize the mixture and natural glycerine is added for its humectants properties.

If you enjoy making mayonnaise you will love making creams and lotions, and by creating them yourself you can be sure that you feed your skin with the natural goodness it deserves. Not only are shop bought creams, balms and lotions expensive, but many contain petroleum based products and other undesirable ingredients.

WHAT IS SKIN?

Skin is the largest organ in our bodies. An average-sized adult has about 2 square meters of skin weighing 2.7 kg and 70 per cent of our skin is made up of water. Our skin protects us from hostile environments, maintains our temperature and helps our immune systems to combat disease. It also communicates sensation and excretes toxins that can affect our general health. In short, our skin is well worth taking care of. Structurally, the skin is made up of three principal layers and a large number of sub-layers. The principal layers are:

Epidermis: the outer layer of the skin (about the thickness of a sheet of paper) – this is the layer we see.

Dermis: this is the thick middle layer containing collagen and elastin which give skin strength and elasticity.

Subcutaneous: this is where fat, nerves and blood vessels live, it is also home to the roots of hair follicles, oil and sweat glands.

WHAT BENEFITS DO CREAMS HAVE?

The basic ingredients used to make natural creams can be divided into three categories:

Humectants: attract water from the dermis and help to maintain moisture in the epidermis. Vegetable glycerine is the most commonly used natural humectant.

Occlusive agents: oils and waxes that moisturize by forming a physical barrier on the epidermis to act against water loss.

Emollients: lubricate and soften the skin by smoothing flaky cells. Natural emollients include shea butter and cocoa butter.

In addition to the above, essential oils and plant extracts, with their nourishing and anti-bacterial properties, are used. These are absorbed through the layers of our skin to help to sooth inflammation and encourage the growth of new skin cells.

TEXTURE

The texture of your creams and lotions, their feel on your skin and their benefits are entirely dependent on the oils and active ingredients you select. The properties of specific oils and other active ingredients are listed on pages 10–14 to help you make a balanced selection for your recipes. Oils, fats and butters containing a high proportion of saturated fatty acids (such as shea and cocoa butter) make heavy creams that sit on the surface of the skin. Less oily creams can be produced using oils such as hemp seed, evening primrose or sunflower oil, which are all absorbed easily.

PRESERVATIVES

Sadly, to date, an entirely natural preservative does not exist. Traditionally, parabens have been used to preserve face creams but their use is controversial and there are safer alternatives available on the market.

Whenever water is introduced into a cosmetic product it is advisable to use a preservative to eliminate bacterial growth. If you intend to sell your creams, you need to guarantee a decent shelf life so the use of a preservative is critical. If you are making creams for yourself without adding a preservative, make in very small batches and store in the fridge.

When selecting a preservative you need to ensure that it is fit for use with the product you intend to make. Some preservatives will not work when the end product has a high pH or where detergent is included in the formula. I recommend using optiphen (phenoxyethanol ethylhexylglycerin) to preserve products as it is effective and does not irritate sensitive skins. The recommended dose is 6 ml preservative per kilogram of product.

In addition to a preservative you should always include an anti-oxidant such as vitamin E in your creams. Whilst the preservative serves to keep the water content free of bacteria, the anti-oxidant reduces the potential of rancidity in the oils.

EMULSIFIERS

Water and oil will not mix and emulsifiers are used to combine them into a stable emulsion. Also known as E-wax, most emulsifiers are vegetable-based and are a combination of polysorbate 20 (made from lauric acid/coconut oil), cetearyl alcohol or ceteareth 20 (both plant-based fatty alcohols).

Most emulsifiers are sold as white waxy pellets which you add to the oil stage of your formula. However, some E-waxes are divided into two parts, one of which you add to the water stage and one to the oil stage. Natural waxes such as beeswax and olive wax also act as emulsifiers, but they will thicken the product and are most commonly used in balms and ointments.

WATER

Use spring or distilled water in your creams and lotions – do not use tap water unless it has been put through a water filter.

ESSENTIAL OILS

Essential oils are added to creams both for their fragrance and their curative properties, and the amount added to a face cream is, on average, between 0.5 per cent and 0.75 per cent and should never exceed 1 per cent. If you are using

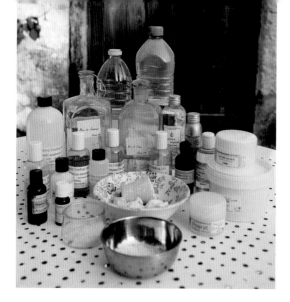

a regular bottle with a dropper and working with 50 g (2 oz) of cream, 0.5 per cent is equivalent to 6 drops of essential oil and 0.75 per cent equals 9 drops of essential oil . However, essential oils must be treated with the greatest respect and the amount we use depends very much on the nature of the oil itself. Aromatherapy is a study of its own so without some in depth research I would suggest that as a beginner you do not exceed 0.5 per cent essential oils in your face cream formula. For fragrance, stick to plant hydrosols or hydrolats (used in place of your water) as an alternative. (See the Essential Oil Selection Chart on page III to get a an idea of which essential oils are best for which skin types.)

EQUIPMENT

Kitchen scales
Whilst you can work with regular kitchen scales you can also buy miniature scales that give you weights of less than a gram (fractions of an ounce). These are incredibly useful for cream makers.

Plastic jug
To weigh your ingredients in.

Medium-sized bowls x 2
Preferably stainless steel for mixing your formula in.

Saucepans x 2
You want to create two bain marie set ups, so ideally you should be able to sit your bowls comfortably on the rim of the saucepans.

Aluminium foil
To cover the bowls while heating.
Thermometer
A digital prober is ideal.
Whisk
An electric whisk will make your life easier.
Measuring spoons
Plastic spatula
Kitchen roll
Washing-up bowl
Vinegar
For sterilizing equipment.
Heat source
Plastic pipettes
For essential oils.
A sponge
For cleaning up.
Assorted containers
For your finished products.

HYGIENE
When making creams, cleanliness and sterility are two major issues. Whilst it is perfectly possible to make creams in your kitchen, you should adopt a regime to ensure that bacteria does not enter your products.

Ensure your hands are clean and your clothes are protected. It's a good idea to not wear woolly jumpers when making creams as these can shed into your product. Tie back your hair or cover with a net or scarf.

Fill a washing up bowl with boiling water for sterilizing, and add two tablespoons of vinegar. Soak all your utensils and jars in this solution for five minutes, rinse thoroughly and then leave them to dry on paper towels (jars bottoms up). Immerse a new sponge in the sterilising bowl and wipe down your work surfaces, then cover with paper towels. Always keep all the equipment you use separate from your day to day cooking equipment.

The biggest cause of bacteria in creams is finger dipping! When applying creams, take them out of the jar with a small spatula. Store your cream making oils in the fridge and keep your essential oils in dark bottles or in a dark cupboard.

MAKING CREAMS AND LOTIONS

Creams are made in four distinct stages:

Stage 1: the oil stage
Melt the oils, waxes, one-stage emulsifiers and cetyl alcohol in a heat resistant jug or stainless steel bowl on a double boiler. Mix until smooth and heat to around 75°C (167°F).

Stage 2: the water stage
Put the water, glycerine, preservative (optional) and/or second-stage emulsifier (if you are using one) into another jug or bowl, mix until smooth then heat to 75°C (167°F) on a second double boiler. Take both saucepans off the heat and pour the oil into the water in a slow stream whilst whisking.

Stage 3: active additives
Once the temperature of your mixture has dropped below 40°c (104°F), add the vitamin E oil, plant extracts or other active ingredients to your cream.

Stage 4: essential oils
Wait until the temperature drops below 30°C (86°F) then add the essential oils. Add a drop of food or cosmetic colourant, if required.

Pour (or use a sterilized spatula to scrape your cream/lotion) into sterilized pots/bottles. Cover with a paper towel until cold, then secure the lids. Do not put the lid on when the formula is still warm as bacteria-attracting condensation can get trapped inside.

CREATING RECIPES

The chart on page 110 gives guidelines for selecting oils. The percentages of ingredients used in your creams should be determined by the desired consistency. To create a rich, heavy cream suitable for dry skin, the total content of fats/oils in your formula should be in the region of 35 per cent. For a general cream, select ingredients for dry skin on the chart but bear in mind that both cocoa butter and shea butter will increase the cream's thickness. For a heavy, mature skin cream, select 35 per cent of

your formula from the oils indicated for mature skin. The ingredients listed for oily skin will give you a lighter textured cream. If you have dry or mature skin but would like a light cream, avoid the inclusion of shea or cocoa butter or reduce the fat and increase the water content until you reach your ideal texture. As an alternative you can replace a percentage of the water content with aloe vera gel, flower waters or witch hazel. Lotions can be made successfully by simply beating up to 50 per cent cold spring water into your completed cream. If you want to colour your cream, add a single drop of food or cosmetic colourant during the final stage.

CALCULATING FORMULATIONS

Recipes for creams, balms and lotions should always be calculated as percentages, so when you add up the percentages for each ingredient in your formula should have a total of 100 per cent.

As you are often weighing very small amounts of ingredients, some cream makers spend a lot of time with tables that convert mililitres to grams or vice versa, but I find it simpler to formulate all cream ingredients in grams to give me 100 g in total, and then to halve or multiply the formula to provide smaller or larger amounts. Sometimes with very small amounts you might find yourself a fraction over or under the 100 per cent, but I have not found this to be an issue. As a rule of thumb, creams and lotions contain:

• 20%–35% oils and fats
• 60%–75% water, gels or hydrosols
• 6%–8% emulsifiers
• 0.5%–1% essential oils

The following are useful guides for ingredients that are difficult to weigh:

• 12-15 drops of essential oil (these vary from oil to oil but the viscosity should give you an idea) = 0.5 g
• 1 ml vitamin E (use a pipette for this) = 1 g
• 12 x drops liquid preservative = 0.5–0.6 g

INGREDIENTS SELECTION CHART BY SKIN TYPE						
BASE INGREDIENTS	OILY	DRY	COMBINED	PROBLEM	MATURE	HIGH SAT ACIDS
Almond (sweet)		√	√	√	√	
Aloe Vera	√	√	√	√	√	
Apricot Kernel	√	√	√	√	√	
Argan		√		√	√	
Avocado	√	√	√	√	√	√
Baobab		√			√	
Borage				√	√	
Black Cumin				√	√	
Coconut (virgin)	√		√			√
Calendula				√		
Carrot seed	√	√	√	√	√	
Castor oil	√			√		
Cocoa butter		√	√	√	√	√
Comfrey				√		
Evening Primrose		√	√	√	√	
Glycerin (veg)		√		√		
Grapeseed	√		√	√		
Hemp seed	√		√	√	√	
Jojoba	√	√	√	√	√	
Macadamia					√	
Melon	√	√	√	√		
Meadowfoam	√				√	
Olive		√		√	√	
Peach Kernel	√	√	√	√	√	
Rosehip seed		√		√	√	
Sea Buckthorn			√		√	
Sunflower oil	√	√	√	√	√	
Shea butter		√	√	√	√	√
Wheatgerm Oil		√		√	√	
Witch Hazel	√	√	√	√	√	
Vitamin E		√		√	√	

SKIN CONDITIONS

On both charts on pages 110–111 I have highlighted oils that are proven to be gentle and, in some cases, helpful to problem skins. Many people, however, look to natural cosmetics for a cure to serious conditions, such as severe eczema or psoriasis, for which there is no known cure. If you suffer from mild forms of these conditions it is likely that your skin will benefit from products that are free from harmful chemicals, but for serious conditions such as dermatitis it is recommended that you seek medical advice.

If you are considering making products for babies, use oils such as borage or calendula, and whilst a chamomile hydrolat could be added in small quantity, avoid the use of essential oils altogether.

INGREDIENTS SELECTION CHART BY SKIN TYPE						
ESSENTIAL OILS & HYDROSOLS	OILY	DRY	SENSITIVE	PROBLEM	MATURE	AVOID DURING PREGNANCY
Chamomile (Roman)		√	√			
Cypress		√				Avoid months 1–5
Eucalyptus	√			√	√	
Geranium	√	√			√	Avoid months 1–3
Grapefruit	√			√		
Helichrysum		√	√	√	√	
Jasmine	√		√			√
Lavender	√	√		√		√
Lemon	√	√			√	
Mandarin	√			√		
Neroli			√			
Palmarosa		√				
Patchouli		√			√	
Peppermint	√			√		√
Rose Absolute		√			√	√
Rose Geranium				√		
Rosemary	√			√		
Sandalwood		√				
Teatree	√	√		√	√	
Ylang Ylang	√	√			√	

BASIC CREAMS AND LOTIONS METHOD

1. Weigh and stir the ingredients for the oil phase in a bowl or heat-proof jug. Weigh and stir the ingredients for the water phase in a separate bowl or jug. Put both on the heat and heat to 75°C (167°F).
2. Pour the oil phase into the water phase in a steady stream, whisking continuously.
3. Once the mixture is cool and thick, add the essential oils, whisk again and scoop into sterilized pots.

1

2

3

CREAMS

ONE OF THE TRUE DELIGHTS OF making creams, lotions and balms is the absence of caustic soda. You can use the very best quality oils with the certain knowledge that their therapeutic properties will remain active.

The following recipes will produce around 100 g of product but you are free to halve or double quantities as you wish. The important thing is that the total of all the ingredients adds up to as close as you can get to 100 g. Use the charts on pages 110–111 to substitute oils according to the particular properties they will bring to your product.

You can also substitute spring water for flower waters, herbal infusions, teas or aloe vera which will add a fluffy texture to your cream. It is a simple balancing act — if you want to add something that isn't in the recipe, be sure to reduce the quantity of another oil or liquid in the recipe by the same amount, and remember that a higher water content means a thinner cream or lotion.

Sleeping Beauty

HEAVY CREAM

This delicious night cream will nourish and soften so you wake up with supple and silky skin.
It's particularly good for dry skin and is fragranced with lavender essential oil, which should
help you sleep well, but use geranium instead if you are at all stressed out.

1 Sterilize all your equipment
and pots. Weigh the
ingredients for the oil phase,
put them in a bowl and mix.
Weigh the ingredients for
the water phase, put them in
another bowl and mix.

2 Put both bowls on separate
bain maries (double boilers),
covering the bowls with silver
foil. Heat both to 75°C
(167°F).

3 Remove from heat and
steadily pour the oil phase
into the water phase in a
continuous stream, whisking
constantly. When the
temperature reduces to 35°C
(95°F) stir in the vitamin E
oil. When the temperature
reaches 30°C (86°F) add the
essential oil blend of your
choice and stir.

4 Pour into prepared jars and
cover with kitchen paper
(paper towel). Apply lids
when cool.

INGREDIENTS

OIL PHASE

12 g (½ oz) jojoba oil

6 g (¼ oz) unrefined cocoa butter

5 g (¼ oz) avocado oil

4 g (⅛ oz) apricot kernel oil

2 g (⅛ oz) beeswax

2 g (⅛ oz) cetyl alcohol

4 g (⅛ oz) E wax

WATER PHASE

50 g (2 oz) spring water

2 g (⅛ oz) glycerine

11 g (½ oz) aloe vera gel

1 g (¹⁄₁₆ oz) preservative

ADDITIVES

1 g (¹⁄₁₆ oz) vitamin E oil

ESSENTIAL OILS

24 drops lavender

VARIATION

Replace the lavender oil with the same quantity of geranium oil for
a soothing scent.

Fragrant Feet

HEAVY CREAM

This cream is a deep rub that is designed to soften rough skin and deodorize and restore your feet at the end of the day. If you have cracked heels, rub generous amounts of the cream into your feet just before you go to bed and sleep with socks on.

INGREDIENTS

OIL PHASE

10 g (½ oz) olive oil
8 g (⅓ oz) shea butter
5 g (¼ oz) virgin coconut oil
5 g (¼ oz) sunflower oil
2 g (⅛ oz) cetyl alcohol
5 g (¼ oz) E wax

WATER PHASE

61 g (2½ oz) spring water
2 g (⅛ oz) glycerine
1 g (¹⁄₁₆ oz) preservative

ADDITIVES

1 g (¹⁄₁₆ oz) vitamin E oil
1 drop colourant (optional)

ESSENTIAL OILS

4 drops tea tree
2 drops rosemary

1 Sterilize all your equipment and pots. Weigh the ingredients for the oil phase, put them in a bowl and mix. Weigh the ingredients for the water phase, put them in another bowl and mix.

2 Put both bowls on separate bain maries (double boilers), covering the bowls with silver foil. Heat both to 75°C (167°F).

3 Remove from heat and steadily pour the oil phase into the water phase in a continuous stream, whisking constantly. When the temperature reduces to 35°C (95°F), stir in the vitamin E oil. When the temperature reaches 30°C (86°F), add the essential oil blend of your choice and colourant, if using, and stir.

4 Pour into prepared jars and cover with kitchen paper (paper towel). Apply lids when cool.

VARIATION

Replace the essential oils with 6 drops of cypress and 6 drops of lavender and add a tablespoon of pumice powder or oatmeal to your cream.

Baby's Bottom

HEAVY CREAM

This rich cream contains a selection of oils that will be kind on a baby's bottom.
It's a good cream to use to prevent nappy (diaper) rash as it will form a light barrier to
protect the skin. I've used one drop of blue and red food colouring for each jar.

1 Sterilize all your equipment and pots. Weigh the ingredients for the oil phase, put them in a bowl and mix. Weigh the ingredients for the water phase, put them in another bowl and mix.

2 Put both bowls on separate bain maries (double boilers), covering the bowls with silver foil. Heat both to 75°C (167°F).

3 Remove from heat and steadily pour the oil phase into the water phase in a continuous stream, whisking constantly. When the temperature reduces to 35°C (95°F), stir in the vitamin E oil. When the temperature reaches 30°C (86°F), add the borage oil and stir.

4 Pour into prepared jars and cover with kitchen paper (paper towel). Apply lids when cool.

INGREDIENTS

OIL PHASE

10 g (½ oz) olive oil

12 g (½ oz) calendula oil

10 g (½ oz) shea butter

2 g (⅛ oz) cetyl alcohol

4 g (⅛ oz) E wax

WATER PHASE

54 g (2¼ oz) chamomile water

2 g (⅛ oz) glycerine

1 g (⅟₁₆ oz) preservative

ADDITIVES

1 g (⅟₁₆ oz) vitamin E oil

4 g (⅛ oz) borage oil

VARIATION

If baby already has a nappy (diaper) rash, replace the borage oil
with comfrey oil and leave out the colourant.

Almond and Calendula Hand Cream

LIGHT CREAM

To make calendula oil, simply fill a half litre (half pint) jar or bottle one third full with calendula petals, top up with olive oil and leave it on a sunny windowsill for a week, shaking from time to time. At the end of the week sieve out the petals and the oil is ready to use.

INGREDIENTS

OIL PHASE

8 g (⅓ oz) almond oil
8 g (⅓ oz) calendula oil
7 g (¼ oz) hemp seed oil
2 g (⅛ oz) wheatgerm oil
2 g (⅛ oz) cetyl alcohol
8 g (⅓ oz) E wax

WATER PHASE

61 g (2½ oz) spring water
2 g (⅛ oz) glycerine
1 g (¹⁄₁₆ oz) preservative

ADDITIVES

1 g (¹⁄₁₆ oz) vitamin E oil

ESSENTIAL OILS

6 drops lavender
4 drops ylang ylang
2 drops rose

1 Sterilize all your equipment and pots. Weigh the ingredients for the oil phase, put them in a bowl and mix. Weigh the ingredients for the water phase, put them in another bowl and mix.

2 Put both bowls on separate bain maries (double boilers), covering the bowls with silver foil. Heat both to 75°C (167°F).

3 Remove from heat and steadily pour the oil phase into the water phase in a continuous stream, whisking constantly. When the temperature reduces to 35°C (95°F), stir in the vitamin E oil. When the temperature reaches 30°C (86°F), add the essential oil blend and stir.

4 Pour into prepared jars and cover with kitchen paper (paper towel). Apply lids when cool.

VARIATION

Try replacing the essential oils with 6 drops of patchouli and 6 drops of geranium.

Aloe Vera Cream

LIGHT CREAM

Gorgeous, cooling aloe vera is a fine additive for your creams and lotions and creates a fluffy texture. Use as a replacement for some of the water content. You can replace the watermelon and baobab oils with almond and jojoba oil, if you prefer.

1 Sterilize all your equipment and pots. Weigh the ingredients for the oil phase, put them in a bowl and mix. Weigh the ingredients for the water phase, put them in another bowl and mix.

2 Put both bowls on separate bain maries (double boilers), covering the bowls with silver foil. Heat both to 75°C (167°F).

3 Remove from heat and steadily pour the oil phase into the water phase in a continuous stream, whisking constantly. When the temperature reduces to 35°C (95°F), stir in the vitamin E oil. When the temperature reaches 30°C (86°F), add the essential oil blend of your choice and stir.

4 Pour into prepared jars and cover with kitchen paper (paper towel). Apply lids when cool.

INGREDIENTS

OIL PHASE

12 g (½ oz) watermelon oil

7 g (¼ oz) baobab oil

2 g (⅛ oz) cetyl alcohol

5 g (¼ oz) E wax

WATER PHASE

40 g (1½ oz) spring water

2 g (⅛ oz) glycerine

22 g (1 oz) aloe vera gel

1 g (1/16 oz) preservative

ADDITIVES

1 g (1/16 oz) vitamin E oil

8 g (⅓ oz) evening primrose oil

ESSENTIAL OILS

12 drops essential oils of your choice

VARIATION

For a refreshing blend use 6 drops each of rosemary and lemon essentail oils, or for problem skin try 4 drops each of mandarin, grapefruit and rose geranium.

Sunflower and Argan

LIGHT CREAM

In France, argan oil is highly prized for its ability to rejuvenate tired skin. Combined here with sunflower and almond oils, this cream has a light texture, is easily absorbed and will keep mature skin soft and supple.

INGREDIENTS

OIL PHASE

20 g (¾ oz) sunflower oil
8 g (⅓ oz) almond oil
6 g (¼ oz) argan oil
2 g (⅛ oz) cetyl alcohol
6 g (¼ oz) E wax

WATER PHASE

55 g (2¼ oz) rose water
1 g (¹⁄₁₆ oz) glycerine
1 g (¹⁄₁₆ oz) preservative

ADDITIVES

1 g (¹⁄₁₆ oz) vitamin E oil

ESSENTIAL OILS

12 drops essential oils of your choice

1 Sterilize all your equipment and pots. Weigh the ingredients for the oil phase, put them in a bowl and mix. Weigh the ingredients for the water phase, put them in another bowl and mix.

2 Put both bowls on separate bain maries (double boilers), covering the bowls with silver foil. Heat both to 75°C (167°F).

3 Remove from heat and steadily pour the oil phase into the water phase in a continuous stream, whisking constantly. When the temperature reduces to 35°C (95°F), stir in the vitamin E oil. When the temperature reaches 30°C (86°F), add the essential oil blend of your choice and stir.

4 Pour into prepared jars and cover with kitchen paper (paper towel). Apply lids when cool.

VARIATION

Try an essential oil blend of 6 drops helichrysum, 4 drops neroli and 2 drops rose or 6 drops geranium, 4 drops lavender and 2 drops lemon.

Flower Milk

LIGHT CREAM

There is something extraordinarily satisfying about collecting flowers from your garden, creating flower water and then whipping it up into a cream. Flower milks are great for daily skin cleansing and can be followed by a splash of undiluted flower water.

INGREDIENTS

OIL PHASE

6 g (¼ oz) almond oil

6 g (¼ oz) virgin coconut oil

2 g (⅛ oz) apricot kernel oil

2 g (⅛ oz) cetyl alcohol

4 g (⅛ oz) E wax

WATER PHASE

75 g (3 oz) flower water (see opposite)

3 g (⅛ oz) glycerine

1 g (¹⁄₁₆ oz) preservative

ADDITIVES

1 g (¹⁄₁₆ oz) vitamin E oil

ESSENTIAL OILS

12 drops essential oils of your choice

2 drops of colourant of your choice

1. Sterilize all your equipment and pots. Weigh the ingredients for the oil phase, put them in a bowl and mix. Weigh the ingredients for the water phase, put them in another bowl and mix.

2. Put both bowls on separate bain maries (double boilers), covering the bowls with silver foil. Heat both to 75°C (167°F).

3. Remove from heat and steadily pour the oil phase into the water phase in a continuous stream, whisking constantly. When the temperature reduces to 35°C (95°F), stir in the vitamin E oil. When the temperature reaches 30°C (86°F), add the essential oil blend of your choice and stir. If you prefer a thinner lotion, dilute with boiled, cooled spring water until the desired consistency is reached.

4. Pour into prepared bottles and cover with kitchen paper (paper towel). Apply lids when cool.

VARIATION

To make lavender milk, use lavender water and essential oil, or substitute both the water and oils for rose or chamomile.

Flower Water

Steam distillation can produce the most wonderful flower waters that can be added to creams and lotions. Lavender, fresh bay leaves and rose petals all make lovely flower waters which can be made easily using a few pots and bowls on your kitchen stove.

1 Put the stock pot on the hob (do not turn on the heat source yet). Place the 'stand' inside the stock pot. Fill the area around and to the level of the stand with petals or herbs. Pour spring water over the petals/herbs to the level of the stand.

2 Place your heatproof bowl right side up on top of the stand. Turn the heat source to high. Put the stockpot lid upside down on top of the stockpot. Fill the inverted stockpot lid with ice.

3 As the water heats up the steam will rise. As it hits the ice the steam will drip from the upside down saucepan lid into the empty bowl inside to make flower water. When the ice melts, empty the saucepan lid and refill it with more ice. Continue the process until all the water at the bottom of the pan has disappeared – take care to not let the pan burn!

4 If you want to preserve the flower water, you will need to add an equal quantity of alcohol (such as vodka) or denatured alcohol. Personally I do not like using alcohol in my creams as it can make them curdle. I prefer to leave my flower water virgin and add a branded preservative during the cream making process.

INGREDIENTS

Spring water

Petals or herbs (fresh or dried)

Jug of ice cubes

EQUIPMENT

Tall stainless steel stock pot with (preferably glass) lid

Heatproof glass or stainless steel bowl that will fit inside the stockpot

Something to stand the bowl on in the pot (you could use another small inverted bowl or even a brick)

NOTE

I haven't included sizes or quantities for the ingredients because it depends how much flower water you want to make. The important thing is that the pot needs to be big enough to hold the bowl on its 'stand' and to allow the pot lid to be placed upside down on the top without leaving any gaps.

BALMS

A BALM IS A GENTLE NON-AQUEOUS cream designed to both protect and heal the skin. It is made very simply by melting together a combination of natural oils, fats and waxes in a double boiler (bain marie) and adding essential oils. Each ingredient is selected for its specific therapeutic property.

In addition to the wide wariety of vegetable oils available, try experimenting with a range of waxes and butters. The bee has been generous enough to supply us with honey, beeswax, propolis and royal jelly, all of which could be included in a balm. (Vegans may prefer to use olive wax, Mexican candelilla wax or and rice bran wax flakes.) You can also include exotic butters in your blends.

Top of the list are cocoa and shea butter but if you can obtain mango, avocado, muru muru, capuçau (from Brazil) or even coffee butter, try these, especially in lip balms. These recipes will make 100 g of product so if that is what you want to achieve, keep the basic numbers the same.

As balms do not contain water you do not need to use a preservative, but you should add 1 per cent vitamin E oil as an anti-oxidant that will protect the oils in the formula from rancidity.

All Purpose Balm

This is a basic recipe that will help to soften and protect the skin. You can substitute the beeswax with candelilla or olive wax, and you can substitute the oils using the chart on page 110 for guidance. You can also infuse your oils with herbs.

1 Sterilize the jars. Weigh all the ingredients. Using a saucepan on a double boiler, heat all the stage 1 ingredients to melting point.

2 Remove the saucepan from the heat and whisk the mixture until it cools to 40°C (104°F).

3 Add the stage 2 ingredients. Mix well. Pour into jars and cover with kitchen roll (paper towel). Apply lids when cool.

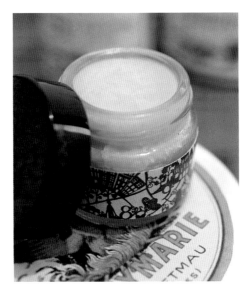

INGREDIENTS

STAGE 1

14 g (½ oz) beeswax
40 g (1½ oz) olive oil
18 g (½ oz) jojoba oil
21 g (¾ oz) calendula oil
6 g (¼ oz) shea butter

STAGE 2

12 drops vitamin E oil
20 drops essential oil
(see Variations below)

VARIATIONS

BRUISING
Replace the calendula oil with comfrey oil
3 drops lavender
3 drops rosemary
3 drops geranium
3 drops arnica

DEEP HEAT RUB
4 drops lavender
4 drops ginger
3 drops eucalyptus
1 drop clove bud

INSECT BITES
6 drops Roman chamomile
6 drops lavender

Gardeners' Balm

This rich antiseptic balm will protect the hands whilst gardening and soothe any scratches. It is also useful as a general antiseptic balm. The watermelon and baobab oils can be substituted with almond and jojoba, and the muru muru butter with another butter of your choice.

INGREDIENTS

STAGE 1

14 g (½ oz) beeswax
40 g (1½ oz) olive oil
24 g (1 oz) watermelon oil
15 g (1 Tbsp) boabab oil
6 g (¼ oz) muru muru butter

STAGE 2

12 drops vitamin E oil
10 drops tea tree oil
5 drops rosemary oil
5 drops eucalyptus oil

1 Sterilize the jars. Weigh all the ingredients. Using a saucepan on a double boiler, heat all the stage 1 ingredients to melting point.

2 Remove the saucepan from the heat and whisk the mixture until it cools to 40°C (104°F).

3 Add the stage 2 ingredients. Mix well. Pour into jars and cover with kitchen roll (paper towel). Apply lids when cool.

VARIATION

To keep the bugs at bay whilst you are working, replace the essential oil blend with 5 drops each of lavender, thyme, eucalyptus and rosemary.

Lip Balms

When making lip balms, texture and taste are very important. We want to achieve a balm that will soften but also protect the lips and for this reason I like to work with chocolatey, unrefined cocoa butter and delicious olive wax.

1 Sterilize the jars. Weigh all the ingredients. Using a saucepan on a double boiler, heat all the stage 1 ingredients to melting point.

2 Remove the saucepan from the heat and whisk the mixture until it cools to 40°C (104°F).

3 Add the vitamin E oil and the essential oil blend. Mix well. Pour into jars and cover with kitchen roll (paper towel). Apply lids when cool.

INGREDIENTS

STAGE 1
28 g (1 oz) olive wax
21 g (¾ oz) calendula oil
20 g (¾ oz) cocoa butter
16 g (½ oz) castor oil
14 g (½ oz) apricot kernel oil

STAGE 2
12 drops vitamin E oil
20 drops essential or fragrance oil of your choice

VARIATIONS

CHOCOLATE VANILLA
Add 1 tsp cocoa powder to the first stage and 4 drops vanilla extract to the second stage for a lip lickable experience.

HONEY BEE
Add ½ tsp honey during stage 1 and use a honey fragrance oil.

MANGO TANGO
Replace the cocoa butter with mango butter and use a mango fragrance oil or geranium essential oil.

WHIPS AND MELTS

THE FOLLOWING RECIPES GIVE YOU the opportunity to seriously indulge yourself and ensure that your skin remains soft and lovely. Run a steaming hot bath, light a scented candle and treat your skin with some of these fantastic products.

The Shea Butter Whip is designed to be slathed on your whole body after a warm bath. It will be quite solid to start with but will melt into your skin. Store in a wide necked jar so you can scoop out handfuls.

Bath Melters are little chunks of moisturizing oils and butters that will make the bath water super soft, and salts from the dead sea are packed with minerals. Try adding them to your bath water or mix them with oil into a skin scrub.

Bath oils offer the best way of adding fragrance to your bath and are extremely simple to make. For the ultimate indulgence, try rubbing yourself all over with a sugar or salt scrub to leave your skin exfoliated and polished.

Shea Butter Whip

This mouth-watering blend of oils and butters is designed to melt on warm (after bath) skin. The shea butter can be substituted with a more exotic butter such as mango or muru muru, and you can also use this as a hair conditioner. This recipe will make 300 g of whip.

1. Sterilize the jars. Weigh all the ingredients. Put the shea butter in a jug or bowl on a double boiler and heat just to melting point.

2. Remove from heat and add the coconut, melon, avocado and vitamin E oils. Mix well. Add your chosen essential oil blend.

3. Stand the jug in a bowl of iced water and whip with either a hand or electric whisk until it has a creamy consistency (you can speed this up by putting it in the fridge for ten minutes before whipping).

4. Scoop into sterilized jars.

NOTE: Shea butter can crystallize due to temperature variations and as a result your finished products may be grainy. To prevent this, heat your shea butter in a double boiler to 82°C (180°F) for 20 minutes before use, then put it in the fridge to solidify again and use as normal.

INGREDIENTS

200 g (8 oz) shea butter

50 g (2 oz) virgin coconut oil

25 g (1 oz) watermelon oil

24 g (1 oz) avocado oil

1 g (24 drops) vitamin E oil

20 drops essential oils (see Variations below)

VARIATIONS

NIGHT OUT
6 drops geranium
6 drops patchouli
6 drops mandarin
2 drops rose

MORNING GLORY
10 drops lime
3 drops sweet orange
3 drops Roman chamomile
2 drops neroli
2 drops jasmine

SLEEP WELL
12 drops lavender
8 drops Roman chamomile

Bath Melters

These little parcels of heaven will dissolve in your bath to soften and fragrance the water. Use latex ice cube trays as moulds as they give you just about the right size of melt. This recipe makes 150 g (5 oz) of product (approximately 24 bath melters).

INGREDIENTS

100 g (4 oz) cocoa butter
20 g (¾ oz) almond oil
10 g (¼ oz) calendula oil
10 g (¼ oz) boabab oil
10 g (¼ oz) apricot kernel oil
20 drops essential oils (see Variations below)

1 Weigh your ingredients. Put the cocoa butter in a jug or bowl and bring to melting point on a double boiler.

2 Remove from heat and stir in the remaining oils. Add your chosen essential oil blend.

3 Pour into an ice cube tray and put in the fridge to harden.

VARIATIONS

FLIRTY
10 drops ylang ylang
5 drops lavender
5 drops sweet orange

SNUFFLY
13 drops rosemary
5 drops eucalyptus
2 drops ginger

Salt and Sugar Scrubs

Before investing in an expensive spa treatment, bear in mind that you can buy the ingredients for salt and sugar scrubs very cheaply and the recipe is really simple – two parts salt or sugar (or a combination of both) to one part oil. Place in a wide-necked jar, add a few drops of your favourite essential oil and shake. That's it! Both the salt and sugar will sink to the bottom of the jar so remember to shake before use.

The subtlety is in which type of salt or sugar you buy. It's not a good idea to go for large, sharp grains as these could be scratchy on the skin, so choose fine or medium grains. Whilst you can make this product using regular table salt, if you want something that will be great for your skin try using a combination of sea salt, dead sea salt and Epsom salts, and the proportion you choose for each really doesn't matter. For sugar scrubs I always use demerara, a medium grained, honey coloured sugar. A teaspoon of honey added to the mix works well. When it comes to selecting oils you could use simple sunflower oil or create a blend yourself using the oil chart on page 110. Jojoba and almond oil are good basic choices.

If you want the scrub to be cleansing as well as polishing, replace a third of the oil with some of your homemade liquid soap, or add a bit of shop bought liquid castile soap. You could also throw in some dried herbs, both for fragrance and for additional exfoliation.

To use your scrub, scoop a handful of the mixture onto a bath mitt or flannel and rub well into the skin in a circular motion, rubbing extra hard on rough areas such as heels and elbows. Rinse off thoroughly and you should feel shiny, tingly and brand new again.

Bath and Body Oil

A good long soak in a bath containing bath oil will undoubtedly help to soften, nourish and moisturize your skin as the heat of the bath helps the body to absorb the oils. You can use virtually any oil or combination of plant oils as a base or you can infuse an oil with dried herbs and benefit from their specific properties. The blend of essential oils you add to your base is the element that makes the bath oil special and also dictates the mood – if you want to relax, refresh or indulge, select your essential oils accordingly. A little essential oil goes a very long way so include the blend at just 1 per cent the weight of your plant oils, or less. You can also use this as a massage oil.

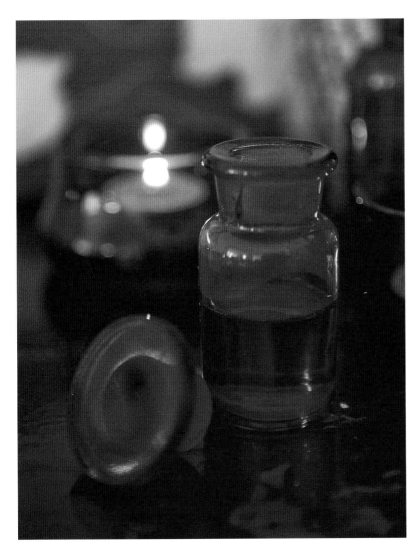

INGREDIENTS

The following is a well balanced base formula:

1 part sweet almond oil
1 part jojoba oil
1 part watermelon oil

Note: The following essential oil blends are for 100 ml/ 3½ fl oz base oil. Adjust quantities accordngly if you are making more or less product.

RELAX

8 drops chamomile
8 drops rose geranium
8 drops lavender

REFRESH

8 drops lemon
8 drops mandarin
8 drops grapefruit

INDULGE

8 drops patchouli
8 drops mandarin
8 drops ylang ylang

SETTING UP A SOAP MAKING BUSINESS

SINCE I SOLD MY SOAP BUSINESS I HAVE dedicated a lot of time to teaching people both the legal obligations and the business and personal skills they will need to make a soap making enterprise successful. Many people who come to me are hobbyists who are addicted to their craft and who feel that running a business is the next natural step, others see a soap making business as a way to work from home. By the end of the course quite a number of the participants decide that the process is far more complicated and requires more time and commitment than they had anticipated, and instead continue making soap as a hobby. Others take the bit between their teeth and go on to build very successful businesses. Your ability to run a successful soap making business lies entirely with you – your circumstances, your skill set and, like any other business, your ability to plan ahead, understand the numbers and most of all to build and market a successful brand. Can you make money from a handmade soap business ? Yes, but only if you are the right person to run it.

Whilst many believe that working for themselves will be an easy option it is far from it. Building any business requires a huge amount of commitment, risk and dedication and unless you thrive on administration this can be a time consuming and tedious task. Soap making is no different. Whilst it is undoubtedly a rewarding, addictive and creative hobby, you could find that the time and energy you need to spend building your business means a great deal less time can be spent actually doing what you love, i.e. making the soap. To run a successful soap business you need to understand all the skills and tasks required, and if you don't have them or can't do them, make sure you know someone who can. Business is about the bottom line, planning is crucial and the ability to cost accurately and keep proper financial records is critical.

You need to adopt the mindset that your soap making is no longer a hobby. Plan your time carefully and be warned, it is very easy for a small business to entirely take over your life – but at least you have all those wonderful bath oils and soaks to relax with.

Soap is made with a caustic chemical which can harm you if used in excess in your products. In addition some botanical ingredients and additives are not recommended for use on the skin. For these reasons it is essential that you ensure that your business is selling safe and desirable products. Different countries have specific laws to ensure you take care of these responsibilities.

EUROPE Within the European Union, soap falls under Cosmetic Legislation. Full details can be found at http://ec.europa.eu/consumers/sectors/cosmetics/documents/guidelines/index_en.htm

USA Providing your soap does not claim to beautify or moisturize the skin it will be classified as a detergent. However, if any claims at all are made it falls under the laws of the Food and Drug Administration (FDA) and full details can be found at http://www.fda.gov/Cosmetics/GuidanceComplianceRegulatory Information/ucm074201.htm

CANADA Soap is classified as a cosmetic. You will find details of the legislation at http://www.hc-sc.gc.ca/cps-spc/person/cosmet/index-eng.php

AUSTRALIA Soap is classified as a cosmetic and great emphasis is placed on labelling and the use of inaccurate claims. You will find full details at http://www.tga.gov.au/docs/html/cosclaim.htm

Whilst complying with the legislation is time consuming, it is designed to ensure that your product is safe and that you can demonstrate complete traceability of its ingredients. You must allot a batch number to each batch of product and you should also keep records of the suppliers and batch numbers of the ingredients you have used.

In practice this means that if you are ever challenged by an individual who believes your product has given him/her a rash, or worse, you have enough information to be able to establish whether or not this could be the case. Be warned, we live in a litigious society and compliance to the legislation is a good thing for everyone. Compliance also demonstrates to your customers that you are a responsible manufacturer who takes his/her craft seriously. Whilst individual countries (within and outside of Europe) have their own additional trading laws that you must comply with, most countries accept that EU legislation is very stringent and the standards are respected throughout the world.

The legislation states that a 'responsible person' must assess and certify any soap or cream formulation that you make for sale. This means you cannot legally sell a single bar of soap – be it to a friend, through a shop, on the internet or via a school fete – unless the recipe is certified. The responsible person needs to be a qualified (and fully insured) cosmetic chemist, toxicologist, pharmacist or GP. I have given a recommendation for a highly competent assessor on page 143.

The above rule applies to all bath products, including melt and pour soap, creams, lotions and bath bombs. Your safety assessor will require the following information from you:

- A list of the ingredients with their INCI names (International Nomenclature of Cosmetic Ingredients). This is usually the Latin name of the ingredient.
- The percentages of each ingredient within your recipe, starting with the largest.
- MSDS sheets (Material Safety Data Sheets) for all your ingredients (ask your supplier for these).
- Colourants with their C.I. numbers.
- Proof from your supplier that any fragrance oils or additives you use comply with IFRA (International Fragrance Association) guidelines.
- A sample of your label (see Labelling, below).
- Knowledge about your step-by-step manufacturing procedures.
- A written step-by-step description of your manufacturing procedures and of your workshop.

Some countries in Europe require that your workshop is completely separate to your living accommodation. This could be a room in your house dedicated to your soap making.

Cosmetic legislation also requires you to keep a comprehensive Product Information File (PIF) for each of your formulations. This should contain your recipe sheet with its allocated name, batch number and date of manufacture. Write on your recipe sheet the supplier of the ingredient and their batch number for it, the size and shape of the finished product, description of any tests you undertook to ensure your product is stable, pH reading if applicable, how you packaged the product and notes on any issues that occurred during manufacture. You should also keep records of who you sold the batch to if at all possible.

LABELLING

The law states that consumers must be given access to information on all of the ingredients within the product at point of sale. If you are wrapping your product then these details must be on the label. If not, they can be stated on a card near the product. The ingredients should be headed 'INGREDIENTS' in caps and listed in INCI format from the largest quantity downwards. This should include water (aqua) but does not need to include sodium or potassium hydroxide as these no longer exist in your final product. Under ingredients, you also need to list allergens that exist within the essential oils if they exceed 0.1 per cent of the total weight of a wash-off product, or 0.01 per cent of a leave-on product. Ask your essential oil supplier for allergen breakdowns.

You are required to state an average weight for your product on the label and this should be followed by the 'e' symbol which must be at least 3 mm high. To ascertain an accurate weight, the law requires that you check your product on 'stamped for trade' scales. If your soap bar weighs between 100–200 g you have a weight tolerance of 4.5 per cent over 40 bars. As soap loses moisture over time, it is a good idea to label your product at 10 per cent less than it actually weighs when you first cut the bars.

Your label also needs to state contact details for your company, your product batch number, date of manufacture and, if it is a cream or a liquid, the open jar symbol with a 'use by' date. If there is any possibility that your soap could be mistaken for food, you also need to put 'DO NOT EAT' in bold, large caps on the label.

CLAIMS

You should take great care to not make any claims on your product label that could be construed as 'medicinal' as this will throw you into complex additional legislation. For example, you cannot say that a product will 'help eczema' unless you have proven this with extensive clinical trials. Whilst you can state that your product contains oils with proven therapeutic properties (e.g. 'includes shea butter for its moisturizing properties'), you should not say that the soap itself is 'moisturizing'. If you are manufacturing soap you must have both public liability and product liability insurance.

SCALING UP

Soap is to a large extent a numbers game. As your profit on each bar is relatively small, you need to sell a lot of soap to make a decent living. When running a business time is at a premium and it takes just as long to make a 20 kg batch of soap as it does to make a 1 kg batch. The first thing you need to do when scaling up is to create a situation where you can make a single, large batch of basic soap and then divide it into separate containers before adding colours, fragrances and additives. This means you may only need to actually make soap one or two days a week.

WORKSHOP

Whether you are working in your kitchen or in a purpose-designed space, make sure you have a wet area for the messy stuff and a dry area for packaging. Also, remember that soap is slippery and if you work on polished floors, fresh soap and essential oils can strip the varnish off. Talk to a plumber about fitting a grease trap under your washing up sink. Fresh soap is fatty and in cold weather fat can solidify and block the pipes. Use paper to wipe off as much soap as possible from your pots and buckets before washing them using washing up liquid.

EQUIPMENT

Replace your small buckets for large buckets and your stick blender with an electric drill with a whisk attachment. Keep your mould size manageable, bearing in mind whatever cutting device you intend to use. There are some very creative cutting solutions on the market which depend to some extent on the size of your initial block of soap. I've provided a link to a UK cutting machine specialist in the stockists section on page 143. Make sure that you choose a mould shape and size that minimizes any waste.

CREATIVE MARKETING

Like it or not, your packaging, brand positioning, name and niche will make or break your business. Here are a few things to think about:

· It is your image that will position you in the market. Some of the most expensive soaps are sold with very minimal packaging.
· There is a lot of competition out there. Focus on a niche market and build a small range which specifically targets it.
· The shape of your soap bar is important. People like a bar that is easy to handle.
· Keep your name short, generic, memorable and easy to fit on bar soaps and bottles. It also needs to be easy to spell for website users. Do the same with your logo.

FIND YOUR NICHE

Look at all age ranges and focus on where you want to go – all age groups and income brackets use soap. Are you aiming at earth mothers or diva shoppers? The upwardly mobile or the already got there? The tourist or the stuck at home with the kids? Picture your customer and list where you think they buy their clothes, what restaurants they go to and what newspaper they read. Your unique selling point could also be based on a rare ingredient you include in your product. Some of the most successful brands have been built on just one main product with a special purpose or identified market, think Coca Cola. Think also of the savings you would make buying in just one set of ingredients in bulk rather than a hundred small bottles that you have paid a premium price for and that will sit on your shelves eating away at your profit.

Do not be tempted to produce numerous varieties of soap – keep your proposition simple and cost effective. The same soap formula can be re-packaged and re-sized to serve several markets.

A flexible packaging solution like paper banding will enable you to personalize soaps with your computer printer. Over 60 per cent of soaps packaged for the gift market do not actually get used – they just sit there for years looking pretty. There are two markets – soap consumers and soap givers. Soap consumers use more, soap givers pay more – cater for both. And remember that male grooming is a buoyant and growing market.

PACKAGING

At the bottom of each of the bar soap recipes I have made suggestions for creative packaging, but if you are designing a range to sell through shops you need a packaging solution that can be handled without damage, projects your image and tells your story. Whilst you are perfectly capable of wowing a store buyer with your products once they get placed in a shop, you only have your product to talk to the customer for you.

If your range includes soaps, creams and lotions, make sure that they all sit together well and that each product is easily identifiable as part of the one brand. Packaging is often more costly than the soap itself so you also need to consider the labour costs. A beautiful, hand wrapped bar of soap can take up to 10 minutes to achieve, so work that out in wages.

DIRECT SELLING

A huge percentage of the population buys soap of one kind or other and yet many soap makers still feel the best outlet for them is a craft market, where there are often other soap makers competing for trade and lots of people who just look rather than buy. Markets are great because they give you an opportunity to see a customer's reaction to your products, but the best markets are the most unlikely ones. At the risk of sounding sexist, consider typical male events like car rallies and imagine how delighted a bored partner

will be when she sees a soap stall oasis she can spend money at. Here are some more places you could try to sell to:
• Guest houses and hotels
• Florist and gift shops
• Health food shops
• Shopping centre (mall) foyers
• Party planning events
• Wedding organizers
• Promotional companies
• In-staff lunchrooms of large corporations
• Internet sites
• Consumer shows where cosmetics are not the focus
• Corporations for their washrooms
• Anywhere where there are lots of people

PR, ADVERTISING AND PROMOTION

You should budget to spend at least 5 per cent of your annual turnover on promoting your company but, whilst repeated advertising can work, your budget would be better spent on establishing your image via your name and logo and a well designed website and/or brochure. Before creating these do lots of research into what other soap makers are doing and then avoid doing the same. An original shape, material or colour combination will help your promotional material stand out from the rest.

The very best form of promotion is PR, which requires the following:
• The ability to write a great press release.
• Good photographs of your products.
• Creating a good network of publicity contacts.
• Sending soap to key people – your product is your cheapest PR resource.
• A great deal of research and hard work.

WEBSITE MARKETING

Soap is not an ideal product to sell on a website as people like to pick it up and sniff it. It is also heavy and therefore costly to mail. If you are starting a website from scratch you also need to understand that unless you invest a great deal of money promoting the site, it usually takes at least six months to build a decent hit rate. If you want to sell via the web, link up with established websites where your product will fit.

INDEX

African Black Soap 81
All Purpose Balm 127
Almond and Calendula Hand
    Cream 118
aloe vera
    Aloe Vera Cream 121
    Seaweed and Aloe Vera 67
Apricot Skin Softener 45
Argile Clay 59

Baby's Bottom 32, 117
Baobab and Marula 74
Basic Liquid Soap Paste 97
Bath and Body Oil 70, 37, 87
Bath Melters 87, 134
Bollywood 87

calendula
    Almond and Calendula Hand
        Cream 118
    Calendula and Goat's Milk 35
Christmas Spice 84

Dead Sea Mud 70

Family Shampoo 101
Fig and Honey 42
Flirty 134
Flower Milk 124
Flower Water 125
Fragrant Feet 114
Fruit Swirls 40

Gardeners' Balm 52, 128
Gardeners' Soap 52
Green Clay and Oatmeal 36

I Do 88

Laurus Nobilis 55, 63, 105
Lavender Provençal 56
Lip Balms 131

Melon and Shea Butter 78
Morning Glory 133

Night Out 133

oatmeal
    Green Clay and Oatmeal 48

Rose and Oatmeal 48

Poppy Seed 51
Provençal 55–63
Purity 32

Rebatched Liquid Soap 105
Rooibus and Wild Honey 77
Rose and Oatmeal 48

Salt and Sugar Scrubs 136
Savon de la Ste Sabine 55, 60
Sea Salt 69
Seaweed and Aloe Vera 67
Shampoodle 102
Shaving Mousse 98
shea butter
    Melon and Shea Butter 78
    Shea Butter Whip 69, 70, 132,
        133
Sleep Well 133
Sleeping Beauty 113
Snuffly 134
Sunflower and Argan 122

FURTHER READING

Handmade Soap Book, Updated Second Edition
Melinda Coss, IMM Lifestyle Books
ISBN 978 1 5048 0022 8

Scientific Soapmaking
Kevin M. Dunn, Clavicula Press
ISBN 978 1 93565 209 0

Making Natural Liquid Soaps
Catherine Failor, Storey Books
ISBN 978 1 58017 243 1

Soap Naturally
Patrizia Garzena and Marina Tadiello
Programmer Publishing
ISBN 978 0 97567 640 0

The Aromantic Guide
Kolbjorn Borseth, Aromantic Ltd
ISBN 978 0 95543 231 6

The Fragrant Pharmacy
Ann Worwood, Bantam Books
ISBN 978 0 55340 397 8

Je cree mes Savons au naturel
Leanne and Sylvain Chevalier, Terre Vivante Editions
ISBN 978 2 36098 007 9

Natural Spa Products
Kolbjorn Borseth, Aromantic Ltd
ISBN 978 0 95543 234 7

RESOURCES

UK

www.soapmakersstore.com
Great range of soap and cosmetic basics.

www.inoviainternational.co.uk
Good when you want to buy in larger quantities.

www.gracefruit.co.uk
Particularly good for those hard to find ingredients.

www.akamuti.co.uk
Specialist African oils, butters & clays.

www.sheabuttercottage.co.uk
More African supplies.

www.sheamooti.co.uk
Distributors of Afrikids' shea butter from Ghana.

www.aromantic.com
Great for your creams and lotion ingredients.

www.makesoap.biz (author's website)
Soap and cream making courses in the UK and France.
Professional soap making moulds.

www.laurelseedoil.com
Wonderful bay laurel oil for Savon d'Alep.

www.dormex.co.uk
Excellent jar and bottle supplier.

www.rockinglambs.co.uk/soap.htm
Great soap cutters.

www.cosmeticsafetyassessment.com
Scott Grainger is a highly qualified chemist and
soapmaker and he is the person to talk to in Europe if
you need cosmetic safety assessments for your recipes.

The author runs soap making business mentoring
and consultancy programmes via www.melindacoss.com
or she can be reached on Facebook at www.facebook.
com/melindacoss.

US

www.snowdriftfarm.com
Great ingredients and lots of recipes and know how.
Also has an online calculator.

www.thesage.com
Another brilliant US supplier with a calculator.

www.moldcreations.com
Suppliers of fancy moulds.

CANADA

www.oshun.ca
Ingredients on a larg scale.

FRANCE

www.aroma-zone.com
Everything you need for soap and creams including
thermometers and mini scales.

AUSTRALIA

www.soapnaturally.org
Supplier links and lots of resources plus a soap
makers forum.

www.newdirections.com.au
Stockist of soap and conmetic making ingredients.

SOUTH AFRICA

www.hexachem.co.za
South African arm of Inovia (see under UK).

INTERNET FORUMS

Captain Ethel's Soap making and Toiletries Resources
www.captainethel.com
Lots of brilliant links for useful suppliers Europe and US.

The following groups are accessed via **www.yahoogroups.com**

UKsoaping
Very helpful group of UK and European soap makers
sharing knowledge.

Liquidsoapers
US group for when the bug really gets you.

Soap_makers
US group. Lots of knowledge and lots of traffic.

ACKNOWLEDGEMENTS

Many thanks to Clare Sayer and Emma Pattison at the publisher
for knocking my idea into shape, applause for Jon Meade and
his great photography and a special thank you to
Carol Benham for correcting my awful 'rithmetic.

A big hug for all my fellow soap makers and clients who have shared
years of ideas and support, in particular Ged Harrison who taught me
the very cold method and de-mystified the thickening of liquid soap.

Finally a big cheer for the team at Makesoap.biz – Juliette, Chris,
Maureen, Jaqui, Sharon and Agnes for enabling me to continue doing
what I love to do best, teaching people how to make and sell soap.